TEDDY BOYS

A CONCISE HISTORY

Ray Ferris and Julian Lord

Milo Books Ltd

Published in December 2012 by Milo Books
© Ray Ferris and Julian Lord 2012

The moral right of the authors has been asserted.

All rights reserved. No part of this publication may be reproduced in any form or by any means without permission in writing from the publisher, nor be otherwise circulated in any form of binding or cover other than that in which it is published and without a similar condition being imposed on the subsequent purchaser.

ISBN 978-1-908479-18-1

Typeset by Jayne Walsh

Printed and bound by
CPI Group (UK) Ltd, Croydon, CR0 4YY

MILO BOOKS LTD
www.milobooks.com

For Shelagh Lord (R.I.P.), Leonard Ferris (R.I.P.)
and the Teds.

From an idea by Paul 'Rambo' Ramsbottom.

CONTENTS

Introduction		5
1	Origins: 1940s–1954	7
2	Heyday: 1955–63	29
Interviews (1)		41
3	Slump: 1964–71	55
4	Revival: 1972–85	59
5	Survival: 1986–Present	83
Interviews (2)		91
Appendix 1: Teddy Boys Worldwide		119
Appendix 2: A Note on the Scuttlers		123
Appendix 3: The Teddy Boys: Facts and Fiction		125
References		127

Introduction

This book is about a much-misunderstood, often-maligned, yet hugely significant cultural phenomenon: the British Teddy Boy. The 'Teds' were not Britain's first youth cult; that honour goes to the scuttlers, vicious gangs of working-class teenagers who terrorised Manchester for thirty years from the 1860s to the 1890s. However, they were Britain's first teenage youth cult of the modern, mass-media-dominated era. As the 1950s, the most important decade for the Teds, fades into the distant twilight in the nation's memory, this book attempts to shed new light and insight onto this most significant of cultural developments, once described as an example of the 'British genius': the new working-class aristocrats, the New Edwardians, or Teddy Boys.

The Teddy Boy style was unique and completely original. Unlike later fashion fads and crazes, it was not manufactured and pushed by the fashion industry; it came from the youths who embraced it, and was their own. Nor was the birth of the Teddy Boy prompted by the advent of rock and roll music, a mistake often made by the media. Rock and roll did not exist in popular form when Britain's first New Edwardian gangs appeared. Some may have decided to adopt the fashion later on because of its association with this new music emerging from America, but a real Teddy Boy will tell you that the arrival of rock and roll was a delightful and not unimportant coincidence, but that was all it was. Anybody can dress up and dance to rock and roll, but this does not automatically make you a Ted, for that is placing the cart before the horse. Being a Teddy Boy is not about music, hairstyles, clothes or

Teddy Boys

dancing; it is about 'being'. Such things, although not unimportant, are merely the external facets reflecting an internal state of mind. Many would argue the point, but such people are, quite simply, wrong.

The Teddy Boys have now been in existence as a coherent subculture for sixty years. So why should they be worthy of inspection? Surely they have had enough publicity and concerned interest in that time? This would be an incorrect conclusion. It is precisely because they have stood the test of time, resisted the changes in fashion and values without flinching, that they require re-examining. What is the inner quality of these men and women that gives them this strength? It is against this most fascinating socio-economic background of massive change, that we should consider the history and impact of the rise of Britain's New Edwardians. This is the story of the Teds, with new research and interviews with some of those who were there, Teddy Boys right from the beginning, years before the advent of rock and roll music.

1
Origins 1940s–1954

The late forties and early fifties was a time of great austerity in Britain, an austerity that only those who lived through it can understand. London and most other major British cities and ports were still suffering the effects of severe bomb damage from the German blitz. Clothes rationing only ended in March 1949. Petrol rationing ended in May 1950. The last rationing of anything, including food, did not stop until 4 July 1954, more than nine years after the end of the war in Europe. The average salary in Britain in 1950 was slightly over £100 per annum, or about £2 per week. To put this in perspective, the cost of a decent semi-detached house in that year would have been around £750, and a portion of fish and chips would have cost you fourpence in old money, or just under 2p today.

However, employment rates were high and the British economy was soon in full swing after the lean years of the thirties and forties, and would remain so right throughout the sixties. Seventy per cent of the working population, which was mostly male, were manual labourers. Britain's middle class was tiny when compared to countries such as the USA, whose middle class by that time had reached sixty per cent of the population: Britain was a country that was overwhelmingly working class in make-up. However, things were about to change, and fast.

The popular dance music of the time was the big-band sound of jazz and swing, the popular dance craze being the jive or lindy hop, a form of dancing introduced into Britain during the war by US servicemen, who were known as GIs,

Teddy Boys

a tongue-in-cheek term that was originally a reference to US Army equipment stamped with the letters GI, standing for 'Government Issue'. Prior to D-Day, the young GIs jived their free nights away with British girls and housewives, many of whose husbands and boyfriends were away at the front, with the result being that the British learned to jive.

Forty thousand British women became 'GI brides' during the Second World War, while thousands of others had romantic liaisons with the visiting Yanks. These US servicemen brought strong American cultural influences with them. Indeed, it is hard to underestimate the impact that the wartime American troops had upon the social life of the country. Britain was no longer the world's superpower, America was. Two world wars had cost Britain a global empire, one million dead and almost every penny she had. A period of questioning and reassessment of Britain's role and purpose in the world began in the late forties, a reassessment that was still ongoing sixty years later. It is fair to say that culturally, there was a loss of confidence, despite the victory over Germany and Japan.

The early Teds thought nothing of learning to jive, it was simply the dance that everybody did. The jive is still one of the dances associated with the Teddy Boys to this day, the other being the bop. But the Teds were jiving years before the advent of rock and roll, a form of music that lent itself perfectly to jiving. American musical influences were already strong in the forties, mainly due to the influence of Hollywood musicals, but by the late forties it is easy to see the early progenitors of rock and roll beginning to make their mark in Britain, with early country blues hits by Hank Williams and the country boogie of Tennessee Ernie Ford. In fashion, the zoot suits worn by civilian-clothed black Americans sported broad-shouldered, knee-length jackets and very baggy trousers. Men's hair styles

Origins 1940s–1954

were generally short but greased back at the sides, sometimes with the hair at the front being combed forwards over the forehead, forming a quiff.

In 1948, as a reaction to the American influence that was changing Britain, something known as the New Edwardian style in men's clothing was reported to be becoming fashionable in the upper and middle classes. This was due to the influence of London fashion houses, notably Hardy Amies and others on Savile Row. It was an extremely sharp style, reminiscent of a more confident yet more class-conscious time, that of the pre-Great War era of Edward VII, and it was in stark contrast to the relaxed and far more casual attitude that the Americans conveyed and which some felt had contaminated the country. Many items of clothing that later became almost exclusively associated with the Teddy Boys can find their origins in World War Two, such as the brushed- suede shoe or chukka (or desert) boot, an item of footwear with a tough crêpe sole originally worn by British soldiers in the deserts of North Africa. They kept the feet warm at night and cool in the day, and demobbed soldiers liked them so much they became a fashion accessory at nightclubs across post-war Britain.

The New Edwardian fashion was promulgated nationally in the daily newspapers and the popular *Picture Post* magazine, inadvertently helping to create the mental conditions required for a quantum leap of thought in Britain's early fifties teenagers. Within a context of great social irony, Britain's working-class youth would take the sharp Edwardian look away from the upper-class elite and mix it with the relaxed attitude of the Americans, to create a synthesis of the best of both worlds. It was a stroke of genius that is unparalleled in the world of the modern subculture, and its reverberations are still being felt.

Teddy Boys

The early New Edwardians pre-dated the rock and roll era by four, possibly even five, years. Bill Haley's 'Crazy Man Crazy', the first recognised rock and roll recording to appear in the national American musical charts, was released in 1953 on London Records and was covered that same year in the UK by bandleader Ted Heath and his orchestra, Teddy Boy favourites of the time. Haley's 'Shake Rattle and Roll' reached number four in the UK hit parade in December 1954, but it was not until 1955 that this 'new' music swept the nation.

At that time, the connection between youth and music was nothing like as well established as it is today. The music that the Teds were listening to before rock and roll took off was the 'big band' sound of the likes of Ted Heath, Johnny Ray and Count Basie, blues 'shouters' such as Big Joe Turner and the boogie-woogie of pianist Sugar Chile Robinson. Robinson, a child piano prodigy, played a fifty-six-day tour of Britain between July and September of 1951. His performance at the Ardwick Hippodrome in Manchester was watched by, amongst others, a teenager called Graham Bowers, from Hyde, Manchester. Now seventy-nine years old, Bowers remembers the audience were wearing tighter than normal trousers, long jackets and brothel-creeper shoes, along with quiffs inspired by the actor Tony Curtis.

The Ted style has been said to have started in London around the Elephant and Castle area of south London, but this appears not to be true; there is much evidence to suppose that the fashion was happening all over the country almost simultaneously. It was merely first reported on in that area of London. In 1952 Leonard Ferris, the father of one of the present authors, was doing his National Service in the Royal Engineers at Yeovil, Somerset. 'When I first went in the Army,' he later told his son, Ray, 'there were many Teddy Boys coming in from London, and all getting their quiffs chopped off

Origins 1940s–1954

and shaved into short back and sides, army regs.' The style was already established before the media picked it up.

The name for the Ted's crêpe-soled shoes, 'creepers', is believed to have been derived from a catchy instrumental that the Teds used to dance to, called 'The Creep', released in the UK in 1954 by Ken Mackintosh and his orchestra. It reached number ten in the charts that January. Creepers, a type of shoe also called beetle crushers because of their thick, flat soles, were developed and marketed by a British company, George Cox, in 1949. This was further evidence of early fashion trends in the development of the new or Neo-Edwardian style amongst pre-rock and roll era teenagers.

In 1953, across all the towns of Britain, the major newspapers reported on this sweeping trend in men's fashion towards what was termed the New Edwardian look. The *Daily Mirror* reported upon the growth of 'zoot suit gangs'. In fact zoot suits originated in Harlem, New York, and were associated with black thirties US jazz culture. The long jacket of the zoot suit resembled the Ted's jacket in that it was very long, and these were at first also referred to as 'drapes' in the US.

Trousers had wide, sixteen-inch bottoms. Often the bottom of trouser legs ended in a 'guardsman's fall' in order to better show the socks, usually white. Jacket lapels were three to four inches wide, and jackets had turn-back cuffs with no velvet on either. (Velvet collars were evident but rare, only gaining in popularity much later on in the mid to late fifties, as velvet added to the expense of a suit, and was seen more often as Britain's prosperity also increased.) Colours were conventionally sombre greys, browns and blacks. Many teenagers were wearing their fathers' jackets that had been taken in. The same applied to trousers, and therefore sixteen-inch-wide bottoms were considered fairly tight, especially as the dominant fashion for men's trousers was still the baggy look left over from

Teddy Boys

the jazz/blues-influenced forties. Oxford bags were typically twenty inches wide or more, therefore sixteen inches would have been considered very tight at the time. There are countless photographs of early Edwardians sporting high-waist peg pants with sixteen- to eighteen-inch bottoms.

Later on the media got the footwear of the Teddy Boys wrong with their reporting of two-inch-thick crêpe soles being worn. The actual thickness was no more than an inch; thicker crêpes did not arrive until the seventies. The Teds also wore Eaton Clubman chukka boots, that had been in evidence since 1947, slip-ons, or chunky brogues and Chelsea boots (not the sixties type). Often Teds would double up the thickness of the soles of their brogues by adding a further layer of leather to give them a more chunky look, something copied by the late-sixties skinheads.

There was also the influence of Western films to consider. This led Teds towards wearing roll collars and brocade waistcoats. The wearing of bootlace ties began in the late fifties and may be directly attributable to the influence of Westerns as television sets became increasingly prevalent in British homes of that period. There was also the influence of Chuck Berry, who wore bootlace ties and velvet roll collars in concerts and films. Shirts were of the high-necked, loose-collar type known as a Mr B. collar. Watch chains were worn for a full Edwardian flavour, and studded belts when worn were a form of statement: they were for use as a weapon, usually worn with jeans when going out fighting in the late fifties. Shirt cuffs were left showing and cufflinks were used. Velvet, if used at all on drape jacket collars, was predominately of the half-back type with some having the velvet inset into the collar, especially in London, and ties were of the 'Slim Jim' type, or an American style Bret Maverick tie, or cravats were worn. Bootlace ties (known as bolo ties in the USA) were only worn in the

Origins 1940s–1954

later fifties, and again may be attributed in large part to the influence of US Westerns. Bootlace ties were in evidence as being worn by those playing the part of Teds (including a very young Freddie Starr) in the 1958 film *Violent Playground*, as were leopard skin print shirts. The wearing of long sideburn whiskers was not in evidence in the early Teddy Boys, and no photographic evidence can be found of them doing so. The early Teddy Boys were mostly too young to grow them anyway. The wearing of sideburns appears to have really only begun after the rise to global fame of Elvis Presley in 1956, and even then the sideburns were only of ear-lobe length, in imitation of Presley. There were one or two eccentrics who took to wearing longer sideburns in the late fifties and early sixties, but there are eccentrics in every era.

Besides their long drape ('drape' from the US, meaning curtains or hanging cloth) jackets with a one-piece back, the original Teds also wore sports jackets, often because they could not afford to buy a tailor-made drape, and peg trousers, with white, yellow or red socks. Pringle-type socks and diagonal and hooped stripes in primary colours were also much in evidence. However, there appears to be no record of Teds wearing fluorescent socks until the late fifties and early sixties. Some opted completely for the style of the Edwardian era (1901–10) itself. There is photographic evidence supporting the wearing of roll-collar jackets from 1953 onwards and roll-collar waistcoats from 1952. Generally, drape jackets initially sported three or four buttons at the front, usually made of bone and later covered in cloth. However there is evidence supporting the wearing of single link buttons dating from 1952. From the photographic and verbal evidence it would appear that no more than perhaps one-fifth of Teddy Boys wore velvet in the fifties.

Early Teddy Boy haircuts were of the Tony Curtis style, or short back and sides with some length left to form a quiff

Teddy Boys

over the forehead, which was also known as a Boston haircut. There is also some sketchy verbal evidence that Teds may have worn the Mohican haircut. This may have been a result of early US influences, as the haircut was worn by elite US paratroops during World War Two. There was also the influence of the 1957 TV series *Hawkeye and the Last of the Mohicans*. US TV programmes, especially Westerns, dominated British television in the fifties. Although it has been reported that some Teddy Boys wore Mohican, or more properly Mohawk, haircuts, it appears to have been a short-lived fashion not adopted generally, and was probably nothing to do with the Teds at all.

From the beginning, the Teds found their homes in gangs. There was safety in numbers. Ted gangs would often distinguish themselves from other Edwardian gangs through a single item of clothing that was uniformly worn by each gang member, such as the colour of socks. By 1953, the Teddy Boy look was beginning to loose its underclass, poverty-stricken roots, and was becoming the height of working-class male fashion. The first 'best dressed Ted' contest was held in the holiday resort of Canvey Island that year. This, however, was just the beginning, for 1955 was to become the year of the Invasion of Britain, and with it, commercial fashion dictatorship was about to rear its ugly head and change the true Edwardian Teddy Boy style.

It was for their perceived violence even more than their fashion, however, that the early Teds were marked out by the newspapers of the day. On 28 January 1953, nineteen-year-old Derek Bentley was hanged for his part in the shooting and killing of a police officer during the attempted robbery of a warehouse in Croydon. Bentley's accomplice, Christopher

Origins 1940s–1954

Craig, was also convicted for his part in the crime, and eventually served ten years in prison. There appears to be some evidence that Craig or Bentley were spivs, cosh boys or early Edwardians. In the 1991 film *Let Him Have It*, when Bentley was hanged, his crêpe-soled shoes were seen to drop from his feet, and had no laces in; this would be accurate due to prison self-harming regulations. However at this time chukka boots were very popular, and it was probably these that he wore. Also he was portrayed wearing a powder-blue full one-piece back drape with flap, turned-back cuffs and pirate pockets. The only difference between this jacket and a true Edwardian-style jacket was that it was double breasted. All the gang in the film were wearing drape-style jackets, brocade waistcoats, crêpes (actually the thicker seventies style, not the originals) and quiffed hair. Overall though, the period detail in the film is superb. The case firmly fixed the problem of juvenile crime into the mind of the public, and the press and media often seemed determined to make Teds and juvenile delinquents synonymous.

In July 1953, the Teds received further bad press when Michael Davies, aged twenty, was convicted of the murder of seventeen-year-old John Beckley during a fight between two groups of youths dressed in Edwardian-style clothing. Although the gang fight that led to the murder began on Clapham Common, it continued outside the park, with Beckley trying to escape on a bus that unfortunately got caught up in traffic. Leaving the bus, he was caught and stabbed several times, dying on the pavement not far from the tube station on Clapham Common's North Side. One Ronald Coleman was described in the *London Evening Standard* as 'the leader of the Edwardians' and his gang, including Davies, was said to have fought with Beckley and three other youths.

Teddy Boys

At the subsequent trial, seven teenage girl witnesses went to court dressed in grey Edwardian-style suits with pencil skirts. These girls referred to the New Edwardians as 'Teddy Boys' and the press picked up on the name. On this evidence, the New Edwardians may have been called Teddy Boys by their peers right from the beginning. In fact the first official mention of the term 'Teddy Boy' occurred on 23 September 1953 in the *Daily Express*. From 1954, this was sometimes shortened to just Teds. So the term Teddy Boy was picked up on by the media but in fact originally came from the streets. In fact the young New Edwardians had been referring to themselves as Teds for some time.

The *Daily Mirror* ran their front page on the case with the headline 'Flick Knives, Dance Music and Edwardian Suits'. Prior to the case, the press had referred to Teds merely as youths dressed in Edwardian clothing. The case was widely referred to as the Clapham Common Murder, but is often referred to by London Teds as the 'bus murder'. The gang Davies was in was called the Plough Boys, due to their members being drawn from the neighbourhood of the Plough Inn next to the tube station. At this time, gangs of Teds got their gang name from the area or local landmark that they were drawn from, such as the gang known as the 'Elephants', who came from the Elephant and Castle area of south London.

Some of these gangs were more 'spivs' than Teds. Post-war rationing and the general shortage of money resulted in an abundance of black-market traders and petty criminals. These were known sometimes as 'wide boys' (men who are 'wide awake' and who live off their wits; the term may also be linked to a style of wide-brimmed felt hat called a wide-awake hat) but more generally as spivs. The true origin of the term 'spiv' is unknown, but might be reverse cockney back-slang for VIPs, the letters 'VIP' standing for Very Important Person. The

Origins 1940s–1954

spiv was a particular type of petty criminal, often a 'fence' or purveyor of stolen goods, who, at the time of rationing, was viewed as providing a service to a population that was sick to death of shortages The spiv was seen almost as a necessary evil in society.

The differences between the spiv and the Teddy Boy were many, and it appears to have been not only that the Teds were teenagers, but also that there was a difference in their *raison d'être*. The spiv wished to appear affluent, and more importantly, socially acceptable in both dress and manner, in order to facilitate his true aim, that of black-market trader or swindler. However, these were not the aims of the Teddy Boys. The spivs were all petty criminals, as that was their means of employment, but many Teds were not necessarily criminals; many had no need to be: affluence was continuing to increase, most conspicuously amongst the young, and by 1957 the average wage had increased to £10 per week. Certainly the spiv would not have resorted to the kind of juvenile crimes that many young Teds went in for, as it would have ended up ruining his business. By the early fifties, the economic circumstances that had produced the spiv in the late forties had ceased to exist, along with rationing, and therefore so did the spiv. This was certainly not the case with the Teddy Boys; quite the opposite. Increasing affluence enabled more teenagers to aspire to being able to afford the clothes, and later on the records, that made up some of the essential possessions of any committed Teddy Boy or Girl.

Very generally then, the spiv was a product of economic circumstance, a working-class economic opportunist, whereas the Teddy Boy was a product of social change, a working-class cultural phenomenon and the first modern sub-cult. There is no way the spivs could be regarded as the latter. However, the media generally saw little difference in the moral corruption that both spiv and Ted posed to civil society, and often interchanged the two terms, a fact that perhaps exposed the depth of ignorance displayed by the establishment as to what was actually happening to Britain's class-ridden society. With hindsight there is the sneaking suspicion that the elite of society deliberately obfuscated the differences between the two. In fairness, however, it should be emphasised that British society had never before faced the phenomenon of an increasingly affluent, better-educated and independently minded working-class youth. The Ted represented colossal social change, and in stuffy, conservative, fifties Britain, this translated into fear. Fear of change meant fear of the Teddy Boy, whether he deserved to be feared or not. Certainly to begin with, he did not, but ignorance is no defence. Like any individual, society will be bound to reap what it has sown. Society, through the press and media, and the courts, was about to sow the wind and it would therefore reap the whirlwind. That whirlwind would come crashing down upon British society a few years later in the form of rock and roll music, with the Teds riding it like the four horsemen of the apocalypse.

In 1950, the number of murders in Britain was 7.9 per million of the population. By 1955 that figure had in fact dropped to 6.3 per million, and by 1960 it had dropped even further to 6.2 per million. The fifties saw the Teddy Boys at their peak in terms of numbers, and at their most conspicuous in the public eye. Considering these statistics, how justified was the public and media panic concerning the crime wave supposedly brought about by the Teddy Boys? It is true that the number of reported indictable offences showed a rising trend beginning in 1954, when the Teddy Boys were beginning their notoriety as supposed thugs and hooligans. However the figure was only 9.4 per thousand of population. It would peak in 1992 at the comparatively

Origins 1940s–1954

staggering figure of 110 per thousand, or almost twelve times greater.

There was in fact a continuous rise in crimes of juvenile delinquency, beginning with and continuing right throughout the Teddy Boy era. It is also known that some Teddy Boys carried out more serious crimes; some were convicted of premeditated robberies of warehouses which they carried out in order to pay for their expensive Edwardian suits, others pimped prostitutes in the West End of London. There can be no doubt on one fact at least though: the fifties was, in terms of the statistical crime analysis, a veritable paradise of peace when compared to later decades, no matter what the prevalent perceptions of the time.

It is impossible for anyone born after 1960 to fully comprehend the crushing weight that the British class system exerted prior to about that date, nor therefore can they fully appreciate what was required to be a rebel Ted in the fifties. The Teds aimed to display their disdain towards the social status quo, and their apparel was their outward symbol of this intent. Initially this was due to the fact that their clothing made them stand apart from the dress of the ordinary, working-class youth who were not Teddy Boys. The Teds were different, and this also was part of their initial primary aim: to appear to be outside the norms of the socially accepted values even if, in reality, some of them may not have been. There was also, initially, the knowledge that the upper classes in London were flirting with the Edwardian style, and it was a sure-fire way of working-class youth making a very important social statement that the upper classes no longer had the monopoly on fashion. Of course, as soon as the fashion became associated with the working classes, the upper class rapidly abandoned the dapper Edwardian style. For the first time ever, Britain's working-class New

Teddy Boys

Edwardians had stolen the limelight in fashion and made it their own monopoly. It was a complete triumph.

Any conscious thoughts of a socio-political nature that may have influenced teenagers to become Teddy Boys seem to have been non-existent, except in a vague and generalised way. They appear to have been aware of their socio-economic status in society, but no more so than teenagers of any previous generation. However, they were aware that the world they were growing up in was a very different one to that of their parents' generation. They appear to have held a belief that theirs was the first generation able to take advantage of freedoms unavailable to previous generations and that they were going to take full advantage of this fact. The decision to live an existential life was not made in any intellectual way but rather was an instinctive and emotional impulse that was difficult to resist. Indeed, many appear to have rejected any intellectual reasoning in this regard except in a very broad sense, as with Peter Carroll's remark, 'We lived for a good time. All the rest was propaganda.' (See Interviews.) There was, for example, no thinking along the lines that the threat of nuclear annihilation played a conscious part in their cognitive processes, although one has to think that the ever-present danger of this occurrence happening must have been of some influence at a subconscious level at least.

Interviews with original Teds show that the answers to the question of what caused people to become Teds appear to be fairly straightforward, and in the following order of priority: the smart appearance of the Teds; the Teds were different; they were making a statement that they were rejecting the conventions of the day and the constraints and repression of the past, including the enforced economic austerity of the immediate post-war period; with most true big band swing music long gone, the post-1954 rock and roll musical

Origins 1940s–1954

explosion inspired many to join the ranks. The combination of all four of the above resulted in their incredible success. (By the seventies, British youth was ready to reaffirm the above four points again, conditions in society being different in the detail but the same at a general level to those pertaining in the fifties. Thus the Teddy Boys, alongside the slightly later New Wave movement, powerfully revived.)

The spiv has been caricatured in the media as typically wearing a well-made, wide-shouldered, double-breasted jacket, often in pinstripe material, but photographic evidence is very sparse; people were hardly likely to have their photo taken with a caption underneath reading 'Picture of a Spiv'! The only real connection between spivs and Teds appears to be that both wore well-made suits and both were frowned upon by mainstream society, although of course many teenagers aspired to high-quality clothing, and the apparent affluence of the spiv, if to nothing else, and it is assumed that the early Teds were no different. However, spivs may have had more than a passing influence upon the young Teds in that they reputedly wore brocade waistcoats and chukka boots, both of which were also worn by the early Teddy Boys. This link was later well captured in the 1991 film *Let Him Have It*, starring Christopher Eccleston. Both spivs and Teds were viewed by middle and upper-class society as being flashy and nasty, and both inhabiting a stereotyped criminal underworld of prostitution, larceny and thuggish behaviour. Illegally owned hand guns, often obtained by servicemen returning from the battlefields of the Second World War, were rife at the time. The ease of access to guns was mentioned during the trial of Michael Davies in the Clapham Common murder case; Davies had previously been convicted of carrying one. Some Teddy Boys also made zip guns that were used in gang warfare.

Teddy Boys

The spiv was technically and primarily a criminal, one who planned his crimes in advance. Most Ted crime however, when it occurred, appears to have been a largely unpremeditated, spur-of-the-moment by-product of the Ted lifestyle (as illustrated in the 1959 book *The Insecure Offenders*, by T.R. Fyvel, which records a Teddy Boy gang throwing a man through a plate-glass shop window for no apparent reason). That lifestyle was the end in itself: to be a Teddy Boy was the goal, with any real planning besides that of the immediate present or very near future being anathema to them. For Teddy Boys, occasionally described as Britain's first mass existentialists, to be a Ted was the definition of their existence, and it is not, as some may think, simply a tautology or a circular pattern of reasoning, thus 'I am a Ted, therefore I truly exist' as opposed to 'I merely exist'. This then raises the questions: what was it, or what did it mean, to be a Teddy Boy and who defined this? Was it the Teds themselves, or the response of those who were not Teds, specifically the media and the authorities that represented the established order of society in general?

The role of self-definition, as opposed to being defined by others, and specifically the media, is an important issue. What then has been the role of the media in redefining what a Ted was or is, and this definition then being accepted by the Teds themselves as legitimate? What was the initial self-perception of the first Teds, before they came to the attention of the media? It is not difficult to answer this question. They were young people out for a good time, but with the additional factor that they were letting the rest of society know it. Whatever mainstream society may have thought about this, the Teds did not care. They had no intention of being stopped. It was thumbs-up to the Teds, and the V-sign to anyone else who disapproved.

How did the early Teddy Boys define themselves? On the evidence of interviews, the job of work they did was a secondary

Origins 1940s–1954

although important element of their self-image, but it was not the ultimate criterion of self-definition; many dropped their apprenticeships and went for higher-wage jobs in order to pay for their suits and more immediate lifestyle. They were first and foremost Teddy Boys, and their job of work was a means to an end and not much else. That end was to be a Ted. These are important questions, if only in order that history does not end up being defined and written by those with an agenda that is, or was, not determined by any desire for historical accuracy: the press, media and the authority that they worked for, that is to say, those who wished to retain the status quo in society, those individuals and institutions wishing to retain social, economic and ultimately, political power.

If this last analysis is an acceptable one, there is the serious question as to the extent to which the Teddy Boys, through a system of social feedback via the press and the media, fell into a trap, by becoming the very demons that they were portrayed as. This recurring systemic social trap was one of the central themes of the 1991 gang film *Boyz N The Hood*. If the answer is yes, then we can be fairly certain that the Teddy Boys not only perceived themselves as victims, but moreover, they were right to do so; they actually were the victims of a press and a society that were already completely geared up for and used to the manipulation of facts in order to best facilitate propaganda during the nation's long struggles against nationalism in the First World War, Nazism during the thirties and forties, and Communism through the fifties and beyond.

There can be no doubt from the press articles of the time, that the fifties Teddy Boy phenomenon was viewed by the wider society as a serious and immediate threat to the moral fabric of society and was dealt with as such. It seems therefore that existentialism was fine when practised by those who had power and wealth, but was held in contempt when practised

Teddy Boys

by those who had neither. Is it any wonder therefore that in the mid-fifties many Teddy Boys were extremely violent, with opposing gangs of London Teds meeting in Brighton for gang fights, especially on bank holidays, predating the Mod–Rocker battles of the sixties by ten years. These Teddy Boys, by sheer weight of numbers, appeared to take over and to terrorise Brighton on their weekend jaunts, pulling communication cords on trains and smashing shop and train windows. There was even a police operation in 1961 called 'Operation Teddy Boy', with newspaper pictures of the police dragging young Teds off trains.

It is a well-understood phenomenon within the study of international relations that countries and societies will often create an internal threat, usually from some minority group or race, where in fact no such threat exists, in order to focus and unite majority opinion upon the seriousness of both the fictitious internal, and the real external, threat. The same trick in reverse is performed by failing governments which, in order to bolster support at home and deflect internal criticism, will deliberately create an external threat where none existed. A good example of the latter was the weak Argentine dictatorship's invasion of the British-owned Falkland Islands in 1982. Ironically, the British victory in that war was a godsend to the weak Thatcher Government, which went on to win the subsequent general election largely as a direct result of the British military victory overseas. Whatever the rights and wrongs of that war, the fact remains that both the fall of the Argentine dictatorship and the 1983 British general election victory for the Conservative Party was partly achieved upon the bones of British and Argentine servicemen.

A comparison may also be useful with the McCarthy witch-hunts that took place in the USA from the late forties to the late fifties. In the case of both the UK and the USA, the pressing

Origins 1940s–1954

external threat right through to the end of the eighties was from communist Russia and China and their allies. The German National Socialists under Adolf Hitler used exactly the same tactic with the Jews and other internal minority groups and races, to very great effect in the thirties right up until Germany's final defeat. To their great credit, the USA recognised the injustice of the victimisation that was taking place against some of its own people because of McCarthyism and acknowledged with great shame what it had done in the name of 'freedom'. In Britain, no such 'Reds under the beds' McCarthyism was possible due to the fact that there were millions of Britons who were socialists and millions of people of differing political persuasions who held enormous sympathy for the peoples of the Soviet Union, a country that had lost over twenty million killed fighting the Nazis in World War Two. (The British Labour Government had even approved the selling of the state-of-the-art Rolls-Royce Nene jet engine to the USSR in 1945, much to the horror of the Americans.)

The Teddy Boys, then, appear to have been the only group in Britain that could be picked on (besides the usual suspects, 'funny-looking' immigrants), and they were an ideal target, their disorganised individuals and gangs being too young and politically ignorant to be able to understand what was being done to them, let alone defend themselves in any meaningful way, shape or form, except with their ubiquitous, yet intellectually useless, flick knives.

Demonised to begin with in the early and mid fifties, then in the sixties made into objects of comedy, the Teds were in the seventies and eighties turned by the media into brightly coloured, cute, cuddly parodies of themselves. Britain's first true modern, apolitical social revolutionaries stood not a chance. To their shame, the British establishment appear to have the nasty habit of never apologising unless forced to. To the eternal credit of the Teddy Boys, they have survived as a small, yet growing, and increasingly organised, coherent movement today.

The entire situation is probably more accurately described by what we will now term here historical social fascism within a bourgeois society, but which many Teddy Boys would term 'bollocks to the system'. Most Teddy Boys are not thick, they are acutely aware they have been made a target, and their long-delayed intellectual fight-back may be only just beginning. Some may argue that the Teds got what they deserved for deliberately making a target of themselves. They may have a point, but their point is also 'bollocks'. On this last then, and not without sympathy, the case is rested.

During the fifties, many people went to the cinema at least once a week. In 1950, the film *The Blue Lamp* was released. It has become the tenth most-watched film in British cinema history. Essentially it tells the story of a humble bobby who, while attempting to prevent a robbery, is shot dead by a rebellious youth. In many respects it was an unfortunate prophecy of things to come, bizarrely paralleling many aspects of the Craig/Bentley murder case of three years later. Although the film was made and released four years prior to the start of the rising trend in crime that began in 1954, considering what was to follow, we should take the film as a landmark in British cinema and, to a much lesser extent, British social history.

In 1953, a British film called *Cosh Boy* was released. The film attempted to address the growing problem of juvenile crime. About a gang of juvenile petty criminals and delinquents, the film ended up using old-fashioned disciplinarian values to deal with the perceived problem, with the main villain ending up with a good old thrashing from an adult whilst the police stood by and turned a blind eye. The term 'cosh boy' was often used by the press when they were referring to Teds, implying that Teds generally were armed and violent thugs.

Origins 1940s–1954

There were a number of other films during this first Teddy Boy era that attempted similar themes, such as *Violent Playground* (1958), in which bootlace ties and leopard-skin printed shirts were in evidence, and the most famous of these for the time, *Blackboard Jungle* (1955), which featured the sound of Bill Haley's 'Rock Around The Clock' over its opening credits. These films dealt with the conflict between rebellious youth and the authority of the adult world. One common element was the existence of at least one evil youngster, usually the gang leader, who had to be confronted and overthrown by the seemingly innocent yet concerned adults in the final scenes, and the gang destroyed. The moral point being made was that crime never pays. However, no matter how hard they tried, the films never quite seemed to grasp or address the deeper significance of why the perceived problem of juvenile crime was on the increase, and left the audience with an uneasy feeling that the problem was essentially unsolvable.

As for the Teds, they simply celebrated the fact that the film *Blackboard Jungle* was made at all by rioting and tearing up cinema seats at theatres all over Britain to the film's opening soundtrack. It was first screened in Britain in the Elephant and Castle, south London, and it was at this theatre that the Teds first rioted. In Blackpool, when the film was shown, Teds rioted and jived over the flower beds all along the famous promenade. In 1956, at the Gaiety in Manchester, a thousand teenagers rioted after seeing the film, many dressed in Teddy Boy suits. The film was eventually banned in many cinemas across the country. However 'Rock Around The Clock', with a guitar break that few popular musicians of today could even hope to match, remains one of the biggest-selling records of all time and was quickly reused in a film of the same name, which sparked even more serious rioting.

2
Heyday 1955–63

In 1955, American rock and roll hit Britain full-on. Rock and roll personified what the Teds were about: an irresistible celebration of youth, energy and rebelliousness. The Teds, in an unassailable strategic position as the country's preeminent youth cult, adopted the new music as their own. The Ted look became the dominant style for British youth, with both the working class and many middle-class youth adopting the hairstyle: the DA, or Duck's Arse. The DA confirmed its position as the most popular hair fashion in 1956 with the appearance of Elvis Presley onto the world stage. Presley dominated the music charts and confirmed rock and roll as the dominant form in popular music.

In 1956, the film *Rock Around The Clock*, featuring Bill Haley and the Comets, premiered at London's Trocadero Cinema. The Teddy Boys embraced this new rock and roll music as theirs, and rioted at this and virtually every other cinema up and down Britain where the film was subsequently shown, often slashing cinema seats with their flick knives. The government and media were outraged and the film was subsequently banned from many cinemas. The media jumped on this phenomenon, placing the new rock and roll music and the Teddy Boys at the centre of all the rioting. Newspapers were filled with pictures of Teddy Boys and girls dancing and jiving outside the cinemas. The police were frequently involved in quelling what was in many instances simply teenage high spirits. There can be no doubt that the media had a big hand in sensationalising the rioting and seat slashing, and thereby

Teddy Boys

simply poured fuel on the smouldering embers of the Trocadero riot, and fanned the flames for what in many instances were obviously copycat riots.

Soon a common sight outside dance halls all over Britain were signs at the entrance stating 'No Edwardian clothing' or simply 'No Edwardians'. Sometimes Teds would slip through the security checks at the entrance by pinning up their jackets to a more orthodox length. As for the music being the cause of the riots, this was rubbish: the music was, and still is, an exciting external expression of inner joy. People riot, not music. Why people really rioted in stuffy fifties Britain is the truly interesting question.

The film *The Girl Can't Help It*, released in the US in 1956 and in the UK the following year, featured the sensational singing star Gene Vincent with his group the Blue Caps, along with Eddie Cochran, Little Richard and other greats, and is widely acknowledged by critics to be the best rock and roll film ever made. The films, the cars and the music set much of the scene for the fabulous fifties. The first teenage revolution, never since equalled on any level whatsoever, the first time ever when teenagers felt totally free from the moral restraints upon their parents' generation and felt able to fully express themselves, was fully underway. For good or ill, the Teddy Boys were at the cutting edge of this revolution in self-expression. Most intellectuals and much of the wider society were running to keep up with events, never mind attempting to honestly understand what was causing all this. The Western world had been caught on the hop, knickers in a twist and no doubt about it.

Indeed the sexual revolution began in the fifties and not, as many would have you believe, in the so-called 'free love' era of the sixties. The fact of the matter is that it was the young working-class Teds who were at the forefront of the sexual

Heyday 1955-63

revolution in Britain. The vast amount of sexual references and innuendo contained within so much of the music of forties and fifties rhythm and blues simply spurred on the Teds in this important area. That sexual revolution merely continued into the sixties, but it was the Teddy Boys and Teddy Girls who led the charge. It was certainly not begun by the 'beat' generation of the sixties, with their hippy notions of 'free love'. As many an honest old hippy will confess today, the concept of free love was often simply a peer pressure ruse used by boys to get sex from girls.

One has to seriously ask the question why nonsense such as 'the sexual revolution began in the sixties' (although it was undoubtedly boosted by the wider availability of the contraceptive pill) is promulgated as truth by so many in the British media? At best they pay lip service to the fifties, or belittle its importance by simply ignoring the decade completely. At worst they will have you believe that rock and roll began in middle-class sixties Britain, if you listen to their drivel for long enough. It is as if they have rewritten history and the fifties Teddy Boys barely existed.

That's not to say the Teds were lacking in notions of morality. Jerry Lee Lewis, the pounding rock and roll piano genius nicknamed the 'Killer', arrived in Britain in May 1958, only to be kicked out of the country amid great publicity for having married his thirteen-year-old cousin. The Teddy Boys were among those outraged by the marriage. It was in fact a culture clash, as marrying young cousins in the Deep South of the US was not that uncommon a practice in those days. So Teds did have a moral conscience after all; what a shocking revelation to the moral majority this must have been! The Teds of course forgave Lewis quickly, and for them the ever stalwart Lewis can now do no wrong. Jerry Lee is currently the only surviving member of Sun Records' 'Million Dollar

Teddy Boys

Quartet', comprising Elvis Presley, Johnny Cash, Carl Perkins and himself. His record 'Whole Lotta Shakin' Goin' On' was chosen to be preserved for eternity in the National Recording Registry in America's Library of Congress.

One important effect of this new-found popularity was that it diluted the style. In the early to mid-fifties, the Edwardian Teddy Boy suit was certainly extreme in its length and tightness of trousers, but one single garment of the outfit stood out more than anything else, and that was the waistcoat, typified in the Colin Donnellan photograph on the cover of this book. Brightly coloured, eye-catching brocade waistcoats and watch chains were abundant, complete with roll collars, flap pockets and small amounts of velvet, giving the wearer an aristocratic look, only to change after 1955. By some of the Teddy Boys, V-necked Fair Isle jumpers were worn, and are much in evidence in photographs from the time. In 1957, a now classic photo of a young Teddy Boy called Bob Corbett, wearing what was at the time labelled as an 'unorthodox' Ted suit, but still wearing a pair of high-waist peg trousers, was published in *Teenage Life* magazine. This particular photo spawned thousands of Teds, who emulated his unorthodox style, with its full velvet roll collar and single link button. This photograph proved a landmark in the further movement of Ted fashion away from its dapper Edwardian origins. Today, the photograph looks to be almost embarrassingly stage-managed, the suit itself a prototype of the more commercial style seen towards the end of the fifties and which became the norm for Teds in the seventies. This photo was very strong evidence that the style was being taken out of the hands of the Teds themselves and was increasingly in the clutches of the fashion industry. Drape jackets became more colourful as the fashion industry seized upon the lucrative style. There was also the influence of cartoons of Teds in the newspapers. There was

Heyday 1955–63

even a Ted character called Ted in the ever popular children's comic the *Beano*, who appeared in the weekly strip 'The Bash Street Kids' from 1958–60.

From the fifties through to the mid-sixties, it was not possible to get fitted jeans: the jeans first had to be put on and then the wearer had to sit in a hot bath and shrink the jeans to fit. This resulted in skin-tight or at least drainpipe jeans. Thus the drainpipe trousers look came more to the fore as the fifties wore on, and this was no less true of the Teds. In March 1960, Max Bygraves had a hit record that reached fifth position in the UK charts. Bygraves' record 'Fings Ain't Wot They Used To Be', in which he sang about 'Teds in drainpipe trousers', 'debs in coffee houses' and youngsters attempting to learn rock and roll guitar, captures admirably, and with great humour, the true spirit of fifties Britain in a way no other record has ever managed to even come close to, and is a long- time Teddy Boy favourite for no other reason than this.

On Sunday, 14 December 1958, a fight broke out between two rival gangs of Teds outside Grey's dance hall on Seven Sisters Road in Holloway, London. In the battle that followed, a chopper, knives, knuckledusters and broken bottles were used. This kind of Teddy Boy fighting was commonplace in towns and cities at the time. The thing that made this particular fight prominent was that one Teddy Boy, Ronald Marwood of Islington, stabbed a police constable to death with an undersea diver's knife, after the constable, Raymond Summers, intervened to stop the fight. A large number of young men were arrested that night, and eleven were subsequently charged with offences ranging from unlawful assembly and intent to disturb the peace to possession of offensive weapons. Marwood himself was questioned by police on the Monday morning after the fight, but was released. He immediately went on the run, but later on turned himself in. During his trial he admitted to stabbing the PC with a knife. Despite his previous clean record and two years' National Service, Ronald Marwood was given the death penalty and was executed by hanging at Pentonville Prison on the morning of 8 May 1959.

One month after Marwood was hanged, a similar gang fight erupted at the Woodward Dance Hall in Barking, Essex, during which Terence Cooney, of the Dagenham Teddy Boys, stabbed and killed Alan Johnson, of the Canning Town Teds. Cooney was convicted but was jailed for life rather than executed; killing a British policeman in the fifties held a special significance.

The period from the 29 August to 5 September 1958, saw a series of events that became known as the Notting Hill Riots. Racial tensions had been running high between the indigenous white population of Notting Hill, west London, and the growing Afro-Caribbean immigrant community. This tension had been further stirred up by the activities of fascist groups such as Oswald Mosley's Union Movement. Also black men were being accused of pimping white women, as if it was any more morally acceptable for white men to pimp. During the riots over 100 people were arrested, two-thirds of whom were white, and many of these, although not all, were Teddy Boys. During one incident at the height of the riots, a large number of men of Afro-Caribbean descent threw a petrol bomb from the upper storey of a building where they were holed up at a large group of white youths, mainly Teds, before charging out into the street whereupon a battle broke out between the two sides involving over a hundred men. The fight went on for some time before the police arrived and broke up the trouble.

With the press blaming the riots upon violent and racist gangs of Teddy Boys, the movement's image was again severely

Heyday 1955-63

tarnished, but with hindsight it can be seen that the Teds once again provided a convenient scapegoat with which the British establishment was able to deflect the problem of institutionalised racism that was without doubt endemic throughout the whole of society. The real victims in the affair were in fact the two groups in society that were perhaps least able to understand what was going on: the poorly educated white and black working-class youth of the inner city. It was they who ultimately paid the price, with stiff sentences of up to five years' imprisonment being handed out by the courts for grievous bodily harm, causing an affray, rioting and possession of offensive weapons. However, the fact is that mud sticks, and all Teddy Boys were tarred with the same brush, a fact that was emphasised in the truly awful, and historically inaccurate, film *Absolute Beginners*, released in 1986. As a result of the riots, the annual Notting Hill Carnival was begun, and continues to this day. Essentially a celebration of Afro-Caribbean culture, it is for some strange reason not attended by Britain's Teddy Boys.

The film *Sapphire* (UK 1959) also set the Teds as racists. In one scene, a gang chase a black man, calling him 'nigger' and attacking him with dustbin lids. The black man gets turned away from refuge in a café by the older white men inside. The film not only portrays Teds as inherently racist but also depicts the wider white society, as represented by the men in the café as being in fear of the Teds, and at the very least, indifferent to the fate of the black man. The point of this scene is well made: let he who is without sin, cast the first stone.

The Teddy Boy phenomenon is without doubt a product of the Western world. To become a Ted is a demonstration of an act of will, and for immigrants from the Third World into Britain to make that demonstration is even more so. It is to announce from the rooftops, 'I am a Teddy Boy, a rebel, and whether I realise it or not, I am a Western man!' Racism

Teddy Boys

between Teddy Boys of differing ethnicities or religions is now almost unknown, something the press and media have ignored for over sixty years. Somewhere in all this is a kind of innate Teddy Boy wisdom: being a Teddy Boy is nothing to do with race, it is a state of being.

Britain had quickly adopted the US music, and was soon producing its own crop of singing sensations such as Billy Fury, Tommy Steele, Vince Eager, Marty Wilde and Cliff Richard and the Shadows. Most of these home-grown stars were inspired by Elvis Presley, although Tommy Steele was more influenced by Bill Haley's music. The Teds were not always impressed with these singers, and many regarded Cliff Richard as a bit of a softy, throwing coins at him on one occasion when he appeared on stage. They were far more impressed by the more masculine image and styles of regularly touring American stars such as Gene Vincent and Eddie Cochran.

There can be no doubt that the influence of the stereotypical masculine, have-a-go US male, as portrayed in countless American movies and TV series, especially Westerns, war films and crime thrillers, firmly set the image for millions of young people in Britain of how a 'real man' should look and behave. The Teddy Boys personified this in spades. To them, well-rounded males do not do drugs, they settle their differences one-to-one, are clean and smart and will do their duty if called upon to pay the ultimate sacrifice by their country. They will, however, show no fear in doing their own thing, living life the way they choose to, and if society and its laws prevent these freedoms, then the law and society is an ass, worthy of contempt. It is easy therefore to see just exactly why the British Teddy Boy gives the V-sign to so much of the British conventional way of thinking. Larger than life,

Heyday 1955–63

driving huge gas-guzzling cars or aspiring to, Teddy Boys have been upholding the tenets of the US constitution and the individual's right to pursue happiness for over sixty years, whether they know it or not. They do not expect thanks for this, and unsurprisingly, they rarely get any, for they never did it for the sake of others in the first place, but for their own. If others are too dim to see what the Teds are really doing, then it is others that have the big problem. Most Teds are true to themselves, which is more than can be said for a lot of others in this world.

Rock and roll and its self-appointed champions the Teds carried on until the early sixties when various US 'teen idols', who often seemed to be called Bobby, popularised a drippy, antiseptic rock and roll mainly aimed at teenage girls. This music took hold for a while, only to be blown out of the water eventually by an English beat group called the Beatles, a four-piece band made up of ex-Teddy Boys who cited Carl Perkins, Elvis Presley, Gene Vincent and Johnnie 'Cry Guy' Ray amongst their greatest influences. John Lennon got the inspiration for his Beatle's haircut when they supported Gene Vincent in Hamburg, Germany. Vincent's hair became shaken down during the act and Lennon copied the look along with the leathers. German art student Astrid Kirchherr, the girlfriend of original Beatles bass player Stuart Sutcliffe, was instrumental in crafting the combed-down hair look. Tragically, Sutcliffe died in April 1962 of a brain haemorrhage believed to have been due to a beating he had taken in January 1961 from Liverpool Teddy Boys. It is also true that Pete Best, the original Beatles drummer, refused to comb out his quiff. Enter Ringo Starr, straight out of Teddy Boy band Rory Storm and the Hurricanes.

Although by the early sixties the Teds had begun to decline in numbers, they had been at the top continuously for about

Teddy Boys

twelve years, which is actually a long time for a single fashion and style to dominate. The Rockers eventually became more numerous as wages began to rise again after a slight recession in 1959, and sales of British motorcycles rose in Britain in the early sixties. The typical attire of the Rocker was: plain leather motorcycle jacket, ice-blue jeans turned up at the bottom and a pair of heavy boots, usually with steel toecaps. A silk scarf, usually white in colour, was used as a muffler. As time moved on, and especially from the seventies to the present, the leather jackets often became personalised with protective metal studs, usually with plastic modeller's paint used to write the name of the particular club, or some other motorbike slogans. Cloth patches bearing motorbike slogans were, and still are, often sewn onto the sleeves of the leather jacket. There is even a film clip from sixties of a Rocker with the words 'Beatle Crusher' painted onto the back of his leather jacket, an anti-Beatles wordplay on the beetle crusher shoe favoured by Teds for many years.

The seaside bank holiday clashes between the Mods and the Rockers were big news in all the national newspapers in the sixties. The truth of the matter was talked about by Pete Townshend, lead guitarist with Mod favourites The Who. In an interview he recalled being in Brighton watching Mods getting chased all over by the Rockers, and claimed he even saw newspaper reporters giving a Mod a leather jacket to wear so that he could be photographed as a 'Rocker' being kicked by Mods. Other incidents like this happened. The Mods were apparently paid £5 and the Rockers £10, so we know who was laughing all the way to the bank. To be fair, many Rockers were big lads in their mid to late twenties, whereas the Mods were usually teenage lads just starting to shave. A lot of these Rockers went on to wear drape jackets in the Ted revival of the seventies.

Heyday 1955–63

The middle to the end of the fifties saw many Teddy Boy gang fights, with sometimes as many as a hundred on either side. Teds sometimes travelled from one town to another fighting in their Teddy Boy gang's name, with names such as the Plough Boys and the Elephant Boys from London, the Dingle Boys from Liverpool and many more throughout the country. In the summer of 1960, the Teds again made the national newspaper headlines. A Ted from Eccles in Salford, and his girlfriend, had been assaulted on Worsley Green in Millbrow, Manchester, by a rival gang from Swinton. The Ted from Eccles had managed to eventually escape by jumping into and crossing a nearby brook, ruining his Edwardian suit. Battle lines were soon drawn, and the following Sunday the Eccles Teds gathered on Worsley Green. The Swinton gang, around forty strong, duly turned up, some arriving in cars. The Eccles Teds, some thirty strong, were waiting. A battle royal then ensued, with fists, and weapons ranging from planks of wood and car starting handles, to bricks and knuckledusters. The battle lasted for about an hour. The police turned up and managed to make over twenty arrests, and some of those arrested were sent down for affray, grievous bodily harm and assault with a deadly weapon. The fight, that became known as the Battle of Millbrow, was unanimously judged to have been a victory for the Teds from Eccles.

The Rockers were the original 'ton-up boys', the café racers of the fifties, and like their Ted brothers in arms they were the first of their kind, and shared a common heritage. Indeed many were, and still are, simply Teds on motorbikes. A lot of sixties Rockers were the younger brothers of fifties Teds and loved rock and roll music. The Rockers' favourite artist was undoubtedly Gene Vincent, partly due to the fact that Vincent wore leathers, and the sixties Granada TV show *Don't Knock The Rock* confirms this.

Teddy Boys

Due to the rising influence of Italian-style suits in the early sixties, winkle-picker shoes became fashionable and were adopted by the Rockers. By the time of the great Ted revival of the seventies, both Teds and Rockers were regularly wearing winkle-pickers. It is a fiction that the Teddy Boys in the fifties wore them and there is no photographic evidence or personal testimony to suggest otherwise. It is yet another fact that the media usually get wrong; the style evolved. The largest organisations of Rockers in Britain today are 'Rockers England' and 'Rockers UK'. The Ace Café on the North Circular Road in London has been frequented by Rockers from the fifties to the present day, and is the Mecca of that movement.

Interviews with Teddy Boys (1)

Joe Goulding, aged seventy-seven, of Swinton, Salford

Prior to 1953, I was in Malaya with the army, but we used to get the newspapers sent out to us. I read all about the Teddy Boys; they were calling them 'Teddy Boys' when I came out of the army in '53. They were well established and started around all the major cities at the same time. There was pretty much instant communication, and the papers rolled out the same news in London and Manchester on the same day, so it was happening everywhere, all over the country at the same time, and everybody knew about it.

I first saw Teddy Boys in Salford in early 1952, there were two of them on Broad Street. I bought my first drape when I was home on leave in '52. The tailor Tom Whitt made it. It was dog-tooth grey, had turn-back cuffs showing a quarter inch of the silk lining, and a one-piece back with no velvet on it. It had four cloth buttons, one straight flap on the breast pocket and straight flaps on the two bottom pockets. If you had velvet on your drape collar, it used to get Brylcreem on it when you danced, which meant you then had to clean it with a special cleaning solution. After a while, the velvet would start to get threadbare. I wore high-waist pegs with no turn-ups on, and they were sixteen- or seventeen-inch bottoms showing just a little of the sock. Lots wore turn-ups, and you could get them with what you call half turn-ups as well, only turned up at the front. Like a Guardsman's Fall. White, yellow and pale-blue socks were in fashion then. If you were a thirty-inch leg you always got

Teddy Boys

trousers that had a twenty-nine-inch leg, so as to show a bit of the sock. All my drapes were finger-tip length.

My shoes were bottle-green lace-ups with a one-inch-thick crêpe sole. After six months of wearing, the crêpe sole used to spread out and they were finished then. They used to get waterlogged and would squelch when you walked in them. Brogues were my secondary choice. I saw Teds wearing chukka boots, and Teds wore Chelsea boots, but they were not the sixties-style Chelsea boots as people think of them today. There were also wedged-toe shoes (flat-toed) and mud-guard shoes. I never saw any Teds who doubled up on their leather soles, but soles of shoes were a lot thicker in those days than they are today.

I had an ordinary waistcoat with no velvet and two pockets. And I had a pocket watch, just a cheap one. My shirt was a cut-away collar type. They used to call them Frankie Laine shirts. It was plain white. Later on I also wore a shirt with frills on, but I was the only one. I used to wear a Slim Jim tie in a Windsor knot. I wore sideburns down to about level with my ear lobes, and I had my hair cut in a DA. We just couldn't grow the sideburns long anyway, we were too young. I never saw any Teds with long sideburns. They were a much later thing.

My second drape was a dark turquoise colour with a full back lining and velvet on the cuffs. It had a three-inch-wide collar. Bigger lads had a four-inch-wide collar because they could carry it. It had flaps on the pockets that could be tucked in for a more casual look. I used to wear braces with my suits. Mud-guard slip-on shoes were worn by some lads. I never saw anyone wearing studded belts. The girls, they used to wear drapes, usually black or oatmeal colour, with a shin-length skirt. Towards the end of the fifties the girls wore flared circle skirts.

The music was Ted Heath, Joe Loss, all the quartets, and

Interviews with Teddy Boys (1)

US blues singers like Sugar Chile Robinson. I'd say the Teds peaked in about '54, definitely before rock and roll came in. There was fighting, lots of it. I used to carry a 'clever stick'; it was a cosh, either slung around my left shoulder on a loop of string or in an inside pocket. You didn't go into town less than three-handed.

I stopped being a Ted in 1955 because I thought the suits were getting too many accessories, like the velvet, and they started looking cheaper. It was getting commercial looking, quick-buck drapes, and not the Edwardian look. Bootlace ties? What the hell have bootlace ties got to do with the Edwardian look? That's when it got cheap, it didn't look right. It used to cost about £25 for an ordinary suit and about £35 for an Edwardian suit, which was very expensive then. I worked nights, so I couldn't go out as much, so I saved my money and could afford the suits. Alec Goodall, Abe Sacks and Tom Whitt were the tailors. They all stopped making Teddy suits in the mid-fifties.

Teds wore sports jackets for casual wear in the daytime, like Terry McGuire. Also slacks. Quite a few wore roll collars, and your velvet collar had absolutely to be hand stitched on to be done properly. The usual colour of the velvet was black or dark blue. Later on I saw maroon and dark-green velvet, that was in about '55. It got too commercial, that's why I packed the Teds in, but I still love the Edwardian style. There is more detail, more thought, in an Edwardian suit. I still have all my suits made in the Edwardian style, even today. I still love the rock and roll.

Winkle-picker shoes came in about 1959–60 but I never saw any Teds wearing winkle-pickers. I'd say virtually all the lads were Teds. In Swinton Palais, the Ritz or the Plaza, you stood out if you weren't a Ted or Edwardian. Half-moon pockets came out about '55 or '56. There was straight piping

Teddy Boys

on the pockets. Windowpane checks, mohair and ghost checks and raindrop flecks were all popular in drapes. I didn't wear raindrop fleck patterns. If I had a black suit it had to have a flash lining, say bright red, and also the tailor would make you a handkerchief out of the same material as the lining. I never saw any Teds wearing earrings. The haircuts were the Caesar (flat top), the Tony Curtis and the South Bank. There were also those lads who had it short at the sides due to them being in the Forces.

The Teds used to wear cheese cutters, a flat-sided cap. I used to wear a small Frank Sinatra trilby that you could get for a shilling. I had a briefcase umbrella, like a businessman's umbrella; no extending handle. I never saw jeans being worn by Teds. Jeans really didn't catch on until the very late fifties, and before that they were considered a work garment. They were mostly bought from Woolworths and Tesco.

Delf Walker was the first [Ted I knew] to have a long-sweep overcoat. They were a bit like the long coats in the Western films. Later on the shorter overcoats took over. The Teds got a reputation for being rowdy, you know, 'look at us, we're Teds', and pub landlords would sometimes throw you out, which was not good if you were out on a date. None of us had a car then. We used to walk or get the bus. Taxis became very wary of picking up Teddy Boys.

I am from Pendleton, a Salford lad from Slater Street. I used to take my shirts to Pendleton laundry for cleaning. I used to go dancing in Eccles, at the Lindale or the Broadway. We used to go to the Astoria on Sunday afternoons and dance as the big bands practised. All the kids used to go and get in cheap on Sundays, and we all loved it. There wasn't the money then. This was pre-1955. Spivs and cosh boys were around when I was a lad. Spivs had double-breasted drapes and brocade waistcoats and wore split-crowned trilbies with their hair in a quiff. They

Interviews with Teddy Boys (1)

hung out in Piccadilly Gardens. They copied the US zoot suit style. It was common for trousers to have twenty-inch bottoms then, that was up until the mid-fifties. Teds' trousers were considered tight in those days.

I saw lots of Teds in Blackpool, they used to come from all over. Yes, I saw Scottish Teds there. We all used to go to the Winter Gardens, and to the revolving café at the front of the fun fair. To me there were very few true Teds in the end. The sixteen-inch high-waist pegs, they were great, but I thought trousers got too tight over time, even around the thighs, and at the knees, the knees started to come out, it looked stupid. It was not the suave Edwardian look that I liked. The Teds are truly British. It was a British thing, the Edwardian style: it was taken from Edward the Seventh's reign. The foreigners have no history of it.

I remember the Rockers [and] I remember seeing 1970s Teds dressed like Showaddywaddy. Their style was, how shall we say, loud. I remember thinking that must be due to commercialism or to a lack of ideas. I became a Ted because it was a complete break from the staid fashions of the past, a break from convention. It wasn't your Easter suit that was plain blue or 'nigger' brown, it was different, it was really smart. I was a Ted from '52 to '55. I was always an Edwardian though. My suits are still made in the Edwardian style. I still am an Edwardian.

Teddy Boys

Frederick Peter Carroll, known as 'Big Peter', aged seventy-four, of Winton, Greater Manchester

I first became interested in the Teddy Boys through fashion, when I read about it in the *Manchester Evening News* when I was about eleven years old. The particular article that first caught my attention was about the Savile Row fashion house Hardy Amies, who were bringing it [the New Edwardian style] out. It was a middle-class thing then, you know, the middle class were wearing it. In the late forties the working class wore any sort of trousers and a muffler, whatever you could get really. In those days the fashions came from Hollywood: wide trousers and white socks.

I bought my first pair of drainpipe trousers about 1952. I think they were fifteen-inch bottoms and possibly had turn-ups on, I can't remember. They were high-waist and I wore them with a belt. Mum took them in for me. I wore one-inch-thick brothel creepers that I bought in 1952. I had what you called a 'South Bank' haircut with a DA at the back, and sideburns later on down to about level with the bottom of my ears. I had no drape, I couldn't afford a drape then. I always wore crêpes.

I got my first Teddy Boy suit in 1954 when I was seventeen. It was what they called a windowpane sky-blue check, with three buttons at the front. It had ordinary cuffs and there was no velvet on it. Finger-tip length, and three-inch collar. The pockets were straight and no flaps on them. The trousers were seventeen-inch bottoms. I wore it with leather shoes, Oxfords with very thick leather soles. Also Chelsea boots, one pair plain and the other pair was a brogue type with a toecap. We wore white socks. I had a roll-collar waistcoat with it. It was my grandfather's originally and I believe it was in an exhibition in Paris. I wore a string tie with a bow in it, or a Slim Jim

Interviews with Teddy Boys (1)

tie, and my shirt was the cut-away collar style with cufflinks. I never saw any pink shirts, all the shirts were white; some were white with a thin pencil-stripe pattern. All the ties had a Windsor knot until the bootlace came in. I didn't wear a fob watch or chain, but a lot did. A lot wore brocade waistcoats. I had a cheese-cutter cap with a stripe in it. It was a kind of silky material, but I didn't wear it with my suit.

I hung out in the Lindale [Eccles, Manchester] Teds. I had heard a load of Teds singing Elvis songs when I was in Blackpool. Elvis set us free. I saw some lads with keys on long chains and some wore studded belts. These were weapons [though] I never saw any bike chains. Some lads wore jeans with their drapes and crêpes, with their collars turned up in the later fifties, but we didn't. We didn't think it looked smart. We were smart. Finger-tip-length drapes were classy. I did see the odd eccentric with a reddish-maroon drape, and there was a lot of blue, and roll collars were popular. I had a suit made with half-moon pockets on. We never saw many primary-coloured drapes. The loudest we saw was pillar-box red, but that was rare. There were also maroon and powder blue. Charcoal-grey suits with raindrop flecks were popular. There was a lot of velvet piping on pockets and cuffs, but everyone was an individual and added their own little touches. Nobody wore pinstripes because that was a class thing, you know, to do with business types.

I'd say the Teds started in 1950. The Vicky Boys [Victorian Boys] tried to make a comeback in 1960. I never saw a Ted wearing winkle-pickers in the fifties, but plenty did in the sixties. Some Rockers wore them with their ice-blue jeans and leathers.

There was loads of velvet in the later fifties, full collars of velvet and a few with velvet-inset collars. I wore suits with three pockets; one ticket pocket, yes. Some had cuffs turned

Teddy Boys

back and some didn't. There were different colours of velvet about, but it was mostly black. I'd say that towards the end of the fifties it got more Showaddywaddy-like. Not many Teds wore tattoos. I also had a flat-top with a DA. I never saw a Mohican [haircut]. The pants got tighter towards the end of the fifties. I also had a one-piece-back drape with a nice silk lining. [The style] went over the top in the seventies. All the young men in Eccles and Salford were Teds; some were semi-Teds. I never saw Teds wear jumpers. Some had overcoats or Crombies with velvet collars, but not many could afford these.

Many wore rings for decorative and destructive purposes. There were plenty of gang fights. I've opened my shoulders once or twice. [Author note: Peter, at six foot three inches and fourteen stone when aged just seventeen, must have been a formidable sight in his Teddy Boy attire.] I was one of the first Teds in the area, but I believe it was starting all over the country at the same time. There were only two of us in the school that were Teds. I'd say the Teds were building up in '53, and by '54 it was sweeping, really fashionable.

The spivs, they were into crime, all of them, but the Teds were a fashion and we were not into crime. I dare say there was one or two like, but we weren't. The older generation saw us as young gangsters. My father didn't like it, and my mum reminded him that he did his thing in the twenties. There were no Teds in other countries [unless you include the Australian and New Zealand 'Bodgies' – the authors], the Teddy Boys had 'Made in Great Britain' stamped all over them.

We all drank. We used to go to the Jazz Club in Manchester. Before rock and roll, I used to listen to Johnny Ray and other crooners. Only a few of us had cars. Those that did have a car, they drove home drunk. We were not as bad as people made out. We called ourselves Teddy Boys and we wanted to be as smart as possible. We lived for a good time,

London gang member Colin Donellan outside a late-night snack bar in October 1953. His suave and sophisticated look has become an iconic image for Teddy Boys of a more recent vintage. *(Photo ©Getty Images)*

A famous *Daily Mirror* headline from September 1953. The Establishment viewed this new youth cult as a serious threat to Britain's class-ridden society. It is difficult for those who were not there to imagine the power of the new rock and roll music upon the young, or the fear of the Teddy Boys engendered in the general public by such headlines.

An early picture of northern Teds: the Ordsall gang in Salford, Greater Manchester. Long Edwardian-style jackets and high-waist trousers are much in evidence. *(Paul Ramsbottom)*

A group of young men drink in a South London pub in 1955. The stocky figure in the middle is Tony Reuter, a hard nut and gang leader who was erroneously labelled 'King of the Teds' by one national newspaper. The press reported that the movement started in the Elephant and Castle area of the capital but photo evidence and personal recollections suggest that its origins were much more diffuse. *(Mirrorpix)*

Classic rock and roll album covers from the mid to late 1950s. The Teddy Boys became inextricably linked to this vibrant and revolutionary sound, even though they predated it by several years.

Tottenham, north London, in the mid-fifties and a resplendent fashion plate is admiringly picked apart by his mates. The youth in the centre has a polka dot tie and four-button Edwardian drape with four-inch collar (no velvet). The others are in similar drapes, with short quiffs and no sideburns.

Mancunian Dennis Burnier Smith astride a motorbike with a pal in 1959. Like many British Teds, Smith idolised the singer Gene Vincent and his rockabilly-oriented style.
(Dennis Burnier Smith)

Rockin' Lewis' Stuart with girlfriend Babs in 1959. Rockin' Lewis was one of the few 1950s Teds who kept the style going through the doldrums of the 1960s. *(Lewis Stuart.)*

The Ordsall Teds, whose style became more casual from the mid-fifties onward. Joe Bay, a black Ted, is on the right. Despite their negative portrayal in the media, particularly after the Notting Hill Riots of 1958, Teds were rarely racist among themselves. *(Paul Ramsbottom)*

The Levenshulme Teds display a melange of styles, from 'ratter', or cheese-cutter, caps to a variety of drapes, jeans and footwear. What had once been a fairly uniform look diverged as the movement matured and as new styles became more widely available in a country formally constrained by cloth rationing. *(Lewis Stuart)*

Young Salford Teds in the Manchester Hotel, Blackpool, adopt a more formal look for a night on the town in July 1960. This photo was taken not long after their infamous mass brawl with rival Teds at Mill Brow. Left to right: Derek, Dave, Bill Evans and Des. *(Bill Evans)*

Bill Evans, aged seventeen, with his girlfriend in 1959. The neo-Edwardian style is still very much in evidence, with Bill sporting a blue brocade waistcoat with a Chinese pattern, a black drape with wide lapels, white shirt with slim-jim tie, grey-blue trousers and highly polished slip-on shoes. The girl is wearing a typical orange circle skirt with a white sash. *(Bill Evans.)*

In stark contrast, a Ted called 'Smokey' sits on a wall in 1960 in classic biker jacket, shades, jeans and crepe-soled shoes. By the early sixties, other fashion influences were coming into vogue such as the leather-clad Rocker look, which many Teds sported for casual daytime wear. *(Lewis Stuart)*

Britain's seaside resorts were hugely popular among young working class adults in the post-War period and became a venue for Teds from different towns and cities to check out each others' fashons. Here the Levenshulme Teds from Manchester ham it up in cowboy hats on a trip to Blackpool. *(Lewis Stuart)*

Some of the founder members of the Salford Bop Cats in 1975. From left to right: the late Tapper Tetlow, 'Corbo' Corbett, Ray Ferris (atop pinball machine), David Gene Vincent, Dave Machin and Paul 'Rambo' Ramsbottom. *(Paul Ramsbottom)*

A mix of northern and southern Teds with a classic Oldsmobile F85 outside London's Lyceum Ballroom in 1976. From left to right: Colin Chippendale, Billy Johnson, Andy Tuppen, Pete 'Spot' Lambert and 'Sunglasses' Ron Staples. *(Billy Johnson)*

October 1988: Frenchman Jean-Marc Chalouni wearing classic neo-Edwardian attire based on the original style of the early British Teddy Boys. The style still has many adherents all around the world. *(Ray Ferris)*

Manchester Teds gather outside the Railway pub in Stockport, Greater Manchester, in January 2011. The picture includes interviewees Bill Evans (third from the left) and Boppin' Brian Spilsbury (fifth from the left). *(Mike Cookson)*

John 'Nidge' Toas, who became a stalwart of the scene during the major rock and roll revival of the early 1970s. *(John Toas)*

'Mad' Mark Mather, from Rochdale, displaying his fine collection of rings to camera in 2011. *(Mike Cookson)*

Teds from all over the United Kingdom gather for a big reunion in July 2011. The return to the original early 1950s neo-Edwardian style of dress is apparent. *(Mike Cookson)*

Teddy Boys co-author Ray Ferris, stalwart of the Salford Bop Cats and founder member of the Manchester Peacock Society, in 2011. *(Mike Cookson)*

Still going strong. From left to right: co-author Julian Lord with interviewees Boppin' Brian Spilsbury and Rockin' Lewis Stuart, and Ted stalwart 'Cockney' Brian Kings. *(Mike Cookson)*

Interviews with Teddy Boys (1)

and all the rest was propaganda.

I think it's great what we all did then. I think it's great what you [the Manchester Teds] are doing now. To me, the Teds, the Ted style, it was the flag of freedom. I am proud to have been a Ted. I am a Ted.

Teddy Boys

Bill Evans, of Winton, Greater Manchester, aged seventy

My dad was born in 1888 and he was a real Edwardian, a period Edwardian, only a young man in the Edwardian era. Big Peter [Carroll] was the first Ted that I knew, that stands out in my mind. Then I was asked by a chap called David to go to the Palais. The music that was popular then was the mambo. At first it was the big bands, then came rock and roll. I still like any big bands and jazz, as well as rock and roll. But I had seen [the Teds] in the newspapers, the same time as when I got pals with Peter in 1955, when I was thirteen and Peter was eighteen, though I had known him since I was eight.

At first it was all forties style, broad shoulders. The Bop Boys had peg trousers with a turn-up. Teds came after the Bop Boys. I'd say then they wore long jackets or coats, as long as box jackets. I used to see Teds here before 1955, first in 1953, often in groups of about ten or so. Raindrop-spotted cloth was popular in drapes, and there was gabardine, barathea and Huddersfield worsted silk, Prince of Wales checks and dog-tooth checks. Some wore raincoats, and some wore overcoats with a velvet collar on them. There were a lot of drapes with small, different-coloured spots on them...The spots were about an eighth of an inch wide, like different-coloured spots on a grey background. I'd say the colours in '55–6 were dark grey, light grey, dark blue, powder blue, navy, black, bottle green and nigger brown. Some wore maroon. Four-button jackets were popular, some with a link button, but some wore two buttons with a link button. The trousers, well some had fourteen-inch, some fifteen, and some sixteen-inch. Some of the trousers had a zip affair at the bottom of the leg so you could alter the width at the bottom. [This in the later fifties – the authors.] I'd reckon the average was about sixteen-inch.

Interviews with Teddy Boys (1)

I wore high-waist trousers with pleats in them. The tailor made a belt with the suit trousers.

I had velvet on one of my drape jackets, but I didn't like a lot, and I preferred no velvet at all. No, I never saw any pink shirts. Shirts had cut-away collars, white was always popular. Some Teds often wore their shirt collars turned up. The ties were the Maverick, Slim Jim and the bootlace ties. I never wore a bootlace, but a fair few did. Most of my mates wore Slim Jims with small knots. Some wore studded belts, and your jeans you wore with your drape during the week. Waistcoats, they were roll collar with four buttons. We used to wear a cheese-cutter cap for casual wear. Some Teds wore box jackets or sports jackets. The girls wore drapes and jackets similar to the men, some with velvet, some without. They wore pencil skirts [that] got shorter over time. Then came the circle skirts with petticoats, like in America. That was in the later fifties.

I met some Scottish Teds in 1960 and they had, I'd say, about a one-inch-square, only small, plaid/check tartan weave in their drapes.

The haircuts, well some had what I call a semi crew cut. I had a haircut like that and also a Tony Curtis. You often had a crew cut and then, as it grew, you styled it into a Tony Curtis. Yes, there were some Teds, only a few, who had Mohican haircuts at the end of the fifties. There were crêpe-soled shoes in 1956, then in '58 they went into the microcellular crêpe style. I had a pair of microcellular crêpes, they had one-inch-thick soles. I wore them with white socks. I also liked black-and-white striped socks with the stripe running down the sock. Fluorescent socks came in the late fifties with Wee Willie Harris, one green and one red, stage socks really, but they had disappeared by the end of the fifties. Slip-on shoes were popular. Microcellular crêpes with a big buckle were popular. There were also monk shoes, a kind of slip-on with

Teddy Boys

a buckle, Oxfords and brogues and also a black suede with a gold buckle. A lot of Teds had sideburns to about ear-lobe length, if they could grow them.

Some Teds carried knives, but I didn't know any of my mates that did. They might have, but no, I didn't know of it if they did. There used to be a lot of scraps. In Tyldesley they had to get the police cars out. There was a big scrap at Mill Brow and it was reported in the *Manchester Evening News* and other national newspapers. There was gang trouble, yes, but people were not as mobile then. You each had your own area, and if a gang came in from another area then there'd be a fight. There was also fighting over girls.

I once saw four lads in Blackpool in 1960 when I was eighteen who had the Victorian style, Vicky Boys they were called. They had brocade waistcoats, watch chains and frilly shirts. I reckon it [the Teddy Boys] died out in 1962.

It annoys me because it appears that the media constantly under-represent the fifties and seem to ignore the incredible importance of it, not only because it was the start of the modern teenage thing but it was also the start of the modern consumer society. The teenagers definitely had much more spending power, and by the mid to late fifties people were buying cars and fridges, and that change was very noticeable. [The media] always seem to think that things began to get going with the sixties but I always say no, that's not right, it was in the fifties. I don't know why they do it, but I know they have the stock footage in their archives because I have seen it on the television but only very occasionally, like footage of the dance halls in the fifties. They don't examine just what an incredible, wonderful atmosphere there was back then, and the rock and roll music with all the different musical styles in it, well to me it has never been beaten. I am not saying it can't be

Interviews with Teddy Boys (1)

beaten, but just that it hasn't. They were unique times, when Jack was as good as his master, clothes were stylish and the records were unsurpassable.

3
Slump 1964–71

In the early sixties, wild rock and roll in the US was in decline. It was being replaced by a seemingly endless succession of cute, teenage, male pop singers such as Fabian and Ricky Nelson. Britain on the other hand was producing some outstanding rock and roll by such artists as Johnny Kidd, Vince Eager and Vince Taylor. Britain had also 'acquired' the US artists Eddie Cochran and Gene Vincent. Despite this immense wealth of talent, however, Britain was about to change musically as well as in fashion. From 1955–63, male youth fashions had become inexorably linked to popular music, much to the advantage of the unholy alliance between Carnaby Street and the giant record labels and greatly to the disadvantage of the Teddy Boys and youth in general. The brief and glorious fashion dictatorship of the proletariat, as personified by the British Teddy Boy, was lost forever. The Beatles helped to kill off the rock and roll/Ted era in 1963. Ironically, when the Beatles split in 1970 fifties rock and roll was set to make its comeback in Britain.

The period 1964–71 witnessed the end of rock and roll's domination of the music charts. Musically, the US welcomed the 'British Invasion' and the domination of the 'Beat Generation' as exemplified by bands such as the Beatles and the Rolling Stones. Teddy Boys and their music were seen as dinosaur relics from an ancient era by the media and the new fashion industry centre, Carnaby Street, in the Soho area of central London. Carnaby Street helped to introduce and define the 'modernist' style (abbreviated to 'mod') during the early to mid sixties and this new

Teddy Boys

fashion spread across large sections of working-class youth. Those taking up the new style were labelled Mods.

The look of the Mod was in stark contrast to the Edwardian style as it attempted to look forward rather than backwards in time for its inspiration. Mod suits were heavily influenced by Italian designs, with short 'bum freezer' jackets and tight trousers. The Teds and Rockers professed to despise the Mods' penchant for wearing eyeliner makeup, riding scooters and taking drugs as an insult to the image of British male youth that they had established in the fifties. No love was lost between the two factions. Violence between the two sub-cults soon broke out, and of course the press latched onto it and blew the factionalism up out of all proportion to the reality. In a feedback loop, the two sides then believed the media hype, and much to the joy and no doubt cheering amusement of the press, made the propaganda a reality. Once again, the working-class youth paid the price for its ignorance of the forces ranged against it. It seems to be a trap each new generation falls into.

A very few Teds, known as Originals because they had been there at the beginning of the movement, alongside a larger, younger group who adopted the style in the late fifties to early sixties, stuck with the Ted look and rock and roll music throughout the sixties. This was especially true in smaller towns and cities, and in some working-class suburbs of the large cities. Ted strongholds emerged, such as South Wales (which in the late sixties produced such bands as Crazy Cavan and the Rhythm Rockers and Shakin' Stevens and the Sunsets), West Yorkshire, the Black Country and the north-east of England. From the early sixties onwards, 'Breathless' Dan Coffey, an original fifties Ted and brother of Mike Coffey of Crazy Cavan, was importing rare rockabilly records on Sun and other labels from the USA and selling them to Teds across Britain. He was instrumental, as

Slump 1964–71

was the Ted movement itself, in promoting this wonderful but largely forgotten music to the world.

In the mid-sixties the Black Raven pub opened up with regular rock and roll nights for the diehard London Teds. It would become an important centre for the later national revival movement of the seventies. It was frequented by Teddy Boys in their late teens, though some Originals did attend. The younger Teds were the main instigators of the revival of the seventies, by which time they were in their late twenties and early thirties and sporting the longer sideburns that had been a popular sixties trend. One of the reasons why the Teddy Boys were a powerful movement was because the leaders were men, case-hardened during their skirmishes in the sixties; the younger Teds of the seventies certainly had good back-up if it came to a confrontation, which it often did. Many of the other cults of the seventies were comprised of teenagers, hence the punk-bashing days of the seventies.

Many of these Teds, who are now in their late sixties, formed their own rock and roll groups, such as Cavan Grogan and Lyndon Needs of Crazy Cavan fame, Sandy Ford and Nigel 'Nigsy' Owen of the Flying Saucers, Graham Fenton of Matchbox and Johnny Fox and Ray Firth of the Riot Rockers. None of these sixties Teds claim to be Originals from the fifties, but they were true ambassadors and great personalities of the seventies rock and roll scene (though Freddie 'Fingers' Lee, the brilliant, piano-pounding rocker was an Original northern fifties Ted). These bands also unwittingly started off the rockabilly movement, Crazy Cavan playing rockabilly style, with guitarist Lyndon Needs doing his own type of country picking and with the band dressed in check shirts, cowboy hats and drapes. The Flying Saucers had their own number, 'Texas Calls You Home', complete with Confederate flags on stage. Then there was Graham Fenton's 'Matchbox',

Teddy Boys

rockabillying to fame on *Top of the Pops*. They all gave a different slant to previous, twelve-bar rock and roll blues.

In late 1968, Elvis Presley's landmark '68 Comeback Special was broadcast on television. Presley, looking sleek and fit in black leather, complete with sideburns and quiff and with some of his original Sun Records musicians backing him, was ready to rock again after years in exile. The scene was being set for its seventies revival, with the King in the vanguard. In April that same year, Bill Haley's 'Rock Around The Clock' was re-released, reaching number twenty in the UK charts. In the same month, Buddy Holly's 'Peggy Sue/Rave On' reached number thirty-nine. Presley hit Las Vegas in 1969, sending audiences into raptures, Haley and the Comets revisited the UK on a tour, and by the end of the decade the Teds had begun to reform their lines, ready to see their musical hero Gene Vincent play live at the London Palladium in November 1969. It was a massive success for Vincent, who tragically died only two years later, on the eve of the great Teddy Boy revival. It is a shame that he never lived to see it, as he would have topped the bill at every venue.

Nineteen seventy-one saw the release of George Lucas' film *American Graffiti*, a highly nostalgic take on the experience of American youth in the early sixties. With its authentic fifties cars and unbeatable rock and roll soundtrack, the film became an instant classic, capturing the youthful spirit of a simpler time and of a lost innocence, before the Vietnam War and the Watergate scandal. It generated massive interest in the era; the fifties became the period for popular music to return to whenever it seemed to lose its way. The great Teddy Boy revival of the seventies had begun.

4
Revival 1972–85

In the early seventies, popular music or 'rock' reached an age (generally recognised by the music industry as dating from the release of Bill Haley's first massive hit, 'Rock Around The Clock', in 1955) where it began to look back at its own past and reassess its roots. There was a nostalgic longing for earlier times, often from artists who were teenagers or children themselves when growing up in the fifties. Music, which was not important in the founding of the Teddy Boys, and more specifically rock and roll music, which was non-existent when the Teds first came into being, became a central pillar in their remarkable national revival.

Don McLean's highly personalised tribute to Buddy Holly, 'American Pie', was a huge hit in 1972. On British TV, specifically the BBC's *Top of the Pops*, 'glam' rock and roll tribute bands Showaddywaddy and Mud had an enormous impact upon teenagers, many of whom had never heard a rock and roll record in their lives. This last fact itself is a damning indictment of the colossal power of the media and music industry. The Rubettes then sparked a revival of interest in doo-wop with their smash single 'Sugar Baby Love', which reached number one in the UK charts in May 1974. The Move's 'California Man', Hank C. Burnette's 'Spinning Rock Boogie' and the band Darts, who supported Jerry Lee Lewis on his 1977 tour of England, all contributed to an upsurge in the numbers of Teddy Boys.

Many of the new recruits had dads and uncles who had been Teds in their youth. This was why so many of them found it

Teddy Boys

easy to get into rock and roll music; they had been brought up with it. Untold thousands of teenagers now began to search out original fifties records. The music industry and the media, always on the lookout for what is new and superficial rather than old and enduring, were unimpressed but could do little to halt the renewed interest in the 'ancient music', even though it was they who reaped the profits from it. Their eternal spectre rose to haunt them with the perennial question: was it possible to make a new sound that is as good as the old rock and roll? No matter how much the industry refuses to answer the question honestly, the answer of course was, and still is in the opinion of the Teddy Boys, a resounding 'No!'

A huge revival concert was staged at Wembley in August 1972, with artists Bill Haley, Little Richard, Jerry Lee Lewis, Chuck Berry and Bo Diddley: the royalty of rock and roll. Upwards of 50,000 attended, many dressed in Ted gear. In September 1973, Bobby 'Boris' Pickett and the Crypt Kickers had a massive hit with their comic rock and roll number 'Monster Mash'. Haley rose again in 1974 with 'Rock Around The Clock', reaching number 12 in the UK charts. Hank Mizell's 'Jungle Rock' reached the number three position two years later. Lured by the prospect of lucrative gigs, American rock and roll stars began regularly touring the UK (including Haley again in 1976), and their music brought tens of thousands of young recruits into the Teds. The Crickets briefly entered the UK charts in 1973 with 'That'll Be The Day', following the release of the film of the same name. In 1975 the film *Tommy* was released, starring Roger Daltrey and his fellow members of The Who. Oliver Reed played a Teddy Boy and Teds featured in the movie, playing the slot machines. All these films and records helped to give the seventies some of that fifties feel.

Revival 1972–85

By the time of the Wembley revival concert, the Ted style of the seventies was already beginning to emerge. The hair was longer and hair lacquer began to replace grease as a means of holding in the DA haircut. Large mutton-chop sideburns, absent in the fifties, were sported and bootlace ties were the norm, as was the increasing use of copious amounts of velvet on collars, pockets and cuffs. The crêpe-soled shoes, however, still had the traditional one-inch soles. The Ted's straight-legged or drainpipe denim trousers were usually flared jeans that had been taken in by hand, as flared jeans were the only option in the shops in 1972. It was also in the seventies that the wearing of tattoos became standard practice, with some Teds opening their own tattoo parlours.

In a time when fashion dictated very long hair, flared trousers, open shirts, medallioned chests and platform shoes, the seventies Teddy Boys were the antithesis of fashion; the complete fashion rebels and, it is obvious with hindsight, rebels with good cause. For the committed Teddy Boy, the opening of old photo albums is never the embarrassment it often is for many of the general population. It is on the contrary a constant source of pride, proof of a mental fortitude denied to others of a weaker disposition. Of course, not all seventies Teds were what they appeared to be. Possibly up to twenty per cent were 'part-time' Teds, who kept their hair long so that they could still go out with their 'smoothie' mates with their centre partings, flared trousers and platform shoes. The genuine Teds of the time called these phonies 'plastics'. Plastics were regarded as traitors to the cause, part-timers lacking the resilience to withstand the ravages of a fickle and changing world. A 'plastic' or 'plastic Ted' is the worst thing one Ted can be called by another. Of course it is an insult that only has meaning within the Ted movement; being called a plastic by non-Teds is a term virtually without meaning.

Teddy Boys

Youth clubs began holding fifties rock and roll discotheques due to the demand from schoolboys and girls. Many youth clubs held exclusive rock and roll evenings and became feeder clubs for Ted pubs as the teenagers got older. Older teens and tail-end fifties/early sixties Teds began forming rock and roll clubs or putting on their own resident bands at their local club or pub, mainly in outlying suburbs. The nightclubs of the city centres came to be viewed as 'for squares only' by the new rock and rolling Teds, who naturally viewed themselves as a teenage elite, preserving a cultural heritage that was under threat and undoubtedly unwanted by the entertainment industry.

The Black Raven pub in London had been a Ted haunt since the mid-sixties, and the Midland Hotel in Manchester opened its doors to the revival in 1972. This was soon reflected all over the UK. The revival picked up greater momentum with the massive chart success of Showaddywaddy and similar revival bands, including Marc Bolan's T. Rex. Bolan, a big Eddie Cochran fan, had a hit with 'I Love To Boogie', which was virtually a straight copy of Webb Pierce's 'Teenage Boogie', with the latter a massive favourite of the Teds in the seventies. Many teens attracted to the Teds and their style favoured bright-coloured drapes that were in tune with the glam-rock fashion of the time. Everybody else was looking flashier, so the Teds flashed it up even more. It is also true that the seventies Teddy Boys were at least as violent as their fifties forebears, and many were determined to live up to that hard-man reputation, come what may.

Happy Days, a US comedy TV series set in Milwaukee in the fifties, hit Britain in early 1974. It sprang directly from the influence and success of the film *American Graffiti*, and was massively popular on both sides of the Atlantic, with regular appearances by female rocker Suzi Quatro, who later became a prominent authority on fifties music and a regular BBC

Revival 1972–85

Radio 2 show presenter. In 1979, Jack Good revived his smash-hit rock and roll TV shows on ITV called *Oh Boy!*, which were first shown on British television in 1958–9. In 1980, a comedy series aired on the BBC called *Hi-de-Hi!* Set sometime in the late fifties in a mythical English holiday camp, one of its most popular characters was Ted Bovis (played by actor Paul Shane), an unlikely-looking, overweight, middle-aged Teddy Boy who was always trying to con people with his streetwise scams. The series was immensely popular and ran for eight years. The popular children's TV series *Grange Hill* also had a Teddy Boy-type character in it called Gripper, who had a violent image; the fifties flavour was still around. In 1985, the film *Back to the Future* was released and became a huge success. Much of it was set in 1955, with American rock and roll music as the backdrop.

A march organised by the Teds was held in London in 1976, with over 6,000 men, women and teenagers from all over Britain, but mainly from London and surrounding towns, marching on the BBC to protest at the lack of authentic rock and roll on the radio. Ten thousand then turned up for the evening's entertainment at Picketts Lock, Edmonton. Another crowd, this time 1,800 strong, marched through Manchester to the BBC offices there in 1977. A couple of coachloads from London ended up fighting with the local Teds when some of the Londoners were seen wearing swastika armbands. A local Ted group called the Salford Bopcats had a mixed-race Pakistani among them, and trouble broke out between the two groups. Four thousand Teds and Teddy girls went on to Belle Vue in Manchester that evening to see bands including Crazy Cavan, the Riot Rockers, and Rockin' Ricky. Both marches produced results, with the BBC acceding to popular pressure and launching a Saturday night radio show called *It's Rock and Roll* that ran for the next three years, hosted by Stuart Coleman.

Teddy Boys

The fighting in Manchester was not unusual. There were many fights in the seventies between Teddy Boys and other youth cults, and Teds also fought each other at times. One stand-up row that became famous was between 'Bonneville Bob', from Oldham, and a young Manchester Ted and well-known amateur boxer in 1976. Bob was ten years older than the boxer, and their fight, outside the Midland Hotel in Burton Road, West Didsbury, lasted for about ten minutes. The older and bigger man put the younger boxer down, but he kept getting up and giving as good as he got. This culminated in two girls who were with Bob hitting the boxer over the head with their stiletto heels. The fight was declared a draw. It was to be the start of a war between the Oldham/Ashton and Manchester Teddy Boys that went on and off for ten years.

In another incident at the same Midland Hotel, a well-known Manchester Ted had an altercation with a rival from Ashton and a Rocker from Oldham. These last two were very dangerous and tough men. One, known as Shotgun Pete, was known to carry a cutlass in his drape jacket pocket. The Rocker was Bonneville Bob, also a tough personality. The Oldham crew threatened to come back to the Midland the following week and the Manchester Teddy Boys formed up for the trouble ahead. They were all at the Midland the next week when the Oldham contingent arrived, dressed in leather jackets, jeans and steel-toecap boots, tooled up and ready to fight. Within minutes, a car came barrelling round the corner, a petrol bomb was hurled from it into the Oldham crew, and one of the men in the car pointed a shotgun. The Oldham crew quickly dispersed and that was the end of the skirmish, though not the end of the war.

It should be mentioned that in the seventies, Teddy Boys wore leather jackets, jeans and winkle-picker boots or shoes, in the style of the Rockers, as casual daytime attire, only

Revival 1972-85

wearing their drape suits when they went out for the evening – unless they were expecting trouble, when daytime wear was the norm but the winkle-pickers were replaced with boots.

Many bands emerged and wrote their own music for Teds in the seventies, inspired by the rockabilly of their predecessors. The foremost of these was Crazy Cavan and the Rhythm Rockers, who are still active today. 'Cavan', as the band is often simply termed, have legendary status with Teds in Britain and with rock and roll fans in every corner of Europe. They would sell their records for £1 a copy at their gigs, and if these had ever been counted by the statisticians, Crazy Cavan would surely have had several chart-busting hits in the UK.

Crazy Cavan played a brand of skiffle-type rockabilly which they called 'crazy rhythm'. They wore drapes, check shirts and jeans, along with cowboy hats. Although Cavan appealed directly to the Teds by singing about them and their lifestyle, with such classics as 'Teddy Boy Boogie' and 'Teddy Boy Rock And Roll', they also helped set the scene for the future rockabilly movement with the likes of 'Rockabilly Star' and 'Rockabilly Rules OK!' Also from South Wales came Shakin' Stevens and the Sunsets. A cousin of Paul Barratt, the agent for all the top seventies rocking acts, who also played sax in the band, Shakin' Stevens went on to massive chart fame in the late seventies and early eighties with hits such as 'This Old House' and 'Green Door'. His success came in parallel with other artists such as Sandy Ford's Flying Saucers ('Texas Calls You Home' and the LP *Planet of the Drapes*), and Graham Fenton's Matchbox ('Rockabilly Rebel'), while a top band from Hull were the Riot Rockers. All these artists were what is known as second-generation Teds, lads who had got into the movement in the early 1960s. It was music made by Teds for Teds. There was also a band of youngsters called The Jets ('Yes Tonight Josephine') from Northampton, their roots firmly set

Teddy Boys

in the strong Teddy Boy background of the DONS, or Drapes Of Northampton Society. The DONS had held a fierce reputation since the fifties. The Jets appealed to both Teds and rockabillies. Another band from late seventies/early eighties was Whirlwind, and both they and The Jets were made up of third-generation Teds, lads who entered the movement in the seventies. There were many other rock and roll bands at the time, too numerous to mention.

As thousands of rock and roll clubs and pubs opened up across Britain, Ted numbers across the country reached perhaps as high as 100,000. London's Lyceum Ballroom regularly received 1,000-plus Teds at its monthly gigs in the mid-seventies, this being mentioned in the *New Musical Express*. West Yorkshire's Bradford Teds and their fearsome gang of over 500 formed a strong alliance with the Manchester Teds in the seventies at the Manchester rock and roll march and the evening dance at Belle Vue. The Bradford Teds became regular visitors to Manchester's Midland Hotel, or the 'Mid' as it was affectionately known, where rock and roll nights were held every weekend. Coaches full of Teds came from all over the country, including London. The Bradford Teds, wearing their cowboy hats, were always one of the largest contingents and there was often standing room only.

The Bradford Teds were also regular visitors to Leeds, which was only ten miles away, and had regular fights with the Leeds Teddy Boys in their clubs and pubs. As Ted historian John van Rheede Toas put it, 'The Bradford Teds were very violent and we were very wary of them in the seventies.' It is on police record that the Bradford Teddy Boys were convicted in the seventies for all types of assaults and affrays, with knives, belts, knuckledusters and even handguns being used in their battles.

In 1979, a documentary-type film called *Blue Suede Shoes* was made at Caister holiday camp, where Teds from all over the

Revival 1972–85

country saw the bands Crazy Cavan, Ray Campi and Freddy 'Fingers' Lee, amongst others. The film was a good portrayal of the Teds at the zenith of their seventies revival. Chris Steel-Perkins and Richard Smith also released their book *The Teds* in 1979. Regarded by many today as a minor classic, it was a bestseller, and was reprinted twenty-three years later. However, the book is thought by most Teds to have shown the movement in a poor light, and it is not highly regarded by the Teds themselves. At the time though, there was nothing else on the market in the way of Teddy Boy literature, and the book, which is largely photographic, does contain a potted history and some analysis of the fifties Teds in its introduction, which places the start of the movement as late as 1954. Although the book has many excellent photos of the Teds taken in the late seventies, it has none from the fifties showing the originals in their authentic Neo-Edwardian suits. A fair number of seventies Teds probably did not even know what the term 'Edwardian' referred to. Most teenagers who became Teds in the seventies were drawn in by the music, following a somewhat different motivation to that behind the genesis of the early Originals.

At the same time as the revival in rock and roll and the Teds was occurring, many films with a fifties youth theme were released, among the most famous being *That'll Be The Day* (1973), *The Lords of Flatbush* (1974), *The Buddy Holly Story* (1978), *American Hot Wax* (1978), *Lemon Popsicle* (1978), *Grease* (1978) and *The Wanderers* (1979). The hit musical *Grease*, although set in a fifties US high school, was musically inaccurate and was essentially a seventies disco-pop vehicle for John Travolta and Olivia Newton-John, contributing to a false stereotype much of the public has of fifties America. The film is hated by many Teds, but it did pull many youngsters into the movement in the late seventies. *That'll Be The Day*,

Teddy Boys

in contrast, brilliantly captured the attitude and spirit of the mid-fifties, with a Ted, played by Ringo Starr, working on fairground rides and conning the punters, and for his troubles being caught and given a good kicking by a gang of Teds. Despite its relatively mild portrayal of Ted violence, the film and its soundtrack, which included original singing stars such as Billy Fury, brought back fond memories for many people, with the sounds of Del Shannon's 'Runaway', Buddy Holly's 'That'll Be The Day' and other great rock and roll tunes that were always played at fairgrounds all over the country whilst people were being spun round on the waltzers by Teddy Boys or Rockers.

In 1977 the sudden death of Elvis Aaron Presley, the undisputed King of Rock and Roll, brought a further influx of youngsters into the Teds. Longtime revival bands such as Shakin' Stevens (number one with 'This Old House' and other hits) and Matchbox (their 'Rockabilly Rebel' reached number eighteen in 1979) rode the wave of the rockabilly musical rediscovery of the late seventies and early eighties, as did the Stray Cats, from New York, USA, whose 'Stray Cat Strut' reached number eleven in April 1981. The Stray Cats had found it impossible to break through the disco/punk/heavy metal dominance in their homeland and were forced to come to Britain in order for their undoubted musical talents to be recognised. Other bands such as the Polecats ('John, I'm Only Dancing') had a definite new wave/punk rock flavour that helped to create the eighties psychobilly scene. But if a Ted audience did not like the band that was playing live, the band often got showered with beer bottles.

There was something of a return to fifties imagery going on, but with a glam-rock style added. From 1973, shoe shops such as Shoe Bonanza began selling wedges with microcellular soles, which were worn by many working-class youths.

Revival 1972-85

You could buy a drape jacket advertised in the *Manchester Evening News* in the mid-seventies for £7, only to receive a blue work-coat with a black velvet collar. How unhappy many Manchester Teds would have been to receive this in the post! They were soon to realise that an expensive tailored suit was the only way forward. To have worn a fifties-style drape suit in the seventies would have gone almost unnoticed, therefore many Teds flashed their style up to extremes. Suits became brighter with more velvet added, quiffs got bigger and sideburns became much exaggerated, reflecting the style of pop stars such as Alvin Stardust, Noddy Holder and Gary Glitter. This was all based upon fifties imagery but was highly exaggerated and blown so far out of proportion by some of the Teds that as the seventies wore on, a new counter-style was being sought by the rebel Teds.

Many younger Teds also became fed up with mental bullying by some of the older Teds, who should have known better. Too often these younger Teds were called 'plastics', meaning fake or false Teds. Instead they became 'Rockabilly Rebels', with Confederate flags adorning the backs of their donkey jackets, wearing check shirts, jeans and steel-toe-cap boots. This clothing was far cheaper than the usually handmade Edwardian suits, and much of it could be obtained at charity shops and the ubiquitous Army and Navy Store. This departure from the Edwardian style began at the end of 1977. Many wore a simple T-shirt, straight jeans and heavy work boots, similar to the sixties Rockers and reminiscent of late-forties US bikers such as the Booze Fighters gang, who were depicted on the sleeve of the LP *Hollywood Rock and Roll*. Some said it was a cop-out, as it was easier to blend in with the fashions of the day. No longer would they have to put up with the aggravations of the squares, and all the fighting that went with it, just for being Teddy Boys and wearing drape jackets.

Teddy Boys

As the new style rapidly evolved, the rebel Teds became known as 'rockabillies' or 'hepcats', and championed US rockabilly music. They attempted to create a more American look, and although some managed to obtain genuine US fifties-style clothing, the majority of their gear was obtained from British shops. Although the hepcats purported to style themselves more upon the fifties American look, they began sporting the very shoes that the original Edwardians wore, namely chukka boots, slip-ons and Oxfords, wearing long box-jacket suits and greasing back their short hair and flat tops in a style similar to the haircuts that Ted conscripts got away with in the 1950s. This contrasted with the majority of the seventies Teds who were sporting large, lacquered quiffs and hair that often hung over the back of their collars. The hepcats obtained high-waist, sixteen-inch peg trousers and often wore long sports jackets bought from charity shops. They were getting turned on to the tunes of Ray Campi, Mac Curtis and others, and looking for all the world much like the first New Edwardians of the early fifties. The style of the pre-commercial hepcat was undeniably sharp.

It should be noted that many of the hepcats were still mates with the Teds, especially on the issue of rockabilly music, due to the huge record collections and unsurpassable knowledge that the Teds possessed. Brian Stetzer, of Stray Cats fame, said in an interview in the *NME* that there was nobody who knew more about rock and roll music than the Teddy Boys. Fusing the Teddy Boy fashion, wearing drapes and crêpes on stage with a rockabilly look, adorning Gene Vincent and Eddie Cochran on their leather jackets, and blasting a blinding fast rock and roll/rockabilly sound, the Stray Cats were cleverly crossing over between the two movements and embracing the teenagers of the day. However, some hepcats sneered behind the backs of the Teds.

Revival 1972–85

The music the hepcats were listening to was the very music that the Teddy Boys had dug so deeply to find in order to add to their already massive record collections. Although many hepcats, but not all, would later deny their Ted origins, a quick glance at their tattoos of Gene Vincent, Eddie Cochran and the cartoon Teds on their arms will confirm the facts. Today large numbers of hepcats have returned to their Teddy Boy origins and are back on the rockin' scene in new drape suits. There was also a difference in the way that many hepcats bopped; a combination of pogo and Ted bopping. To many, the hepcat style of dance looked bizarre and out of place in an Edwardian club. There was also a marked difference in attitude between the two factions. The hepcats tended to stand around looking cool, aloof and vaguely uninterested, even bored, whereas the Teds tended to jive, bop and rock their nights away.

The numbers of hepcats rose steadily, increasing dramatically when Carnaby Street got hold of the emerging style on the back of rockabilly music hitting the charts in the early eighties. The term 'rockabilly' is a combination of words representing two musical styles: 'rock and roll' (itself a combination of country music and rhythm and blues) and 'hillbilly'. With an influx of glue-sniffing punk rockers, the 'psychobillies' soon emerged. With the media adding the suffix 'billy' onto each new artificial fad name it could think of, the rockabilly/hepcat scene quickly descended into a completely meaningless quagmire of 'sillybillies', and many original hepcats, disgusted at this development, returned to traditional suburban venues, leaving the high street fashion victims to dominate the trendy city centre nightclubs such as Manchester's Berlin. Even at the height of the rockabilly trend in the early eighties, however, hepcat numbers never came close to exceeding those of the Teds.

During the seventies, the great style of the early New Edwardians had become so bastardised and distorted that, with

Teddy Boys

hindsight, this breakaway movement was bound to happen. There were simply too few Original Teds left to educate the seventies generation into the ways of the true style of the early New Edwardians, and for many it must be said, the music was the most important feature of the revival. In addition, the Originals were fighting against the forces of fashion and the fashion media, and the preconceptions many young Teds held because of those same forces were simply impossible to overcome. However, the conclusions are inevitable: it is undeniable that the rockabilly/hepcat movement started in Britain, springing directly from the Teddy Boy movement, and is as British as the Teds themselves.

Before 1983, perhaps three-quarters of those in the rockabilly/hepcat movement were made up of former young seventies Teddy Boys and girls that were not media influenced and trendy. After 1983, perhaps a quarter of the rockabilly/hepcat movement were more of the trendy fashion types. Even the original rockabillies were not keen on this development. Frequenting certain clubs in London along with punks, northern soul and Mod types, and psychobillies, these fickle trendy 'kats' disappeared within a few years of the end of the rockabilly fashion craze. In the early to mid-eighties in Manchester's Berlin night club, trendy people thought it was cool to play a 'bit of rockabilly'. The Teds at this time thought this was a joke, knowing that the true meaning of their scene had been obliterated in these places.

As the scene began to split along almost tribal lines, many Teds became very disillusioned, so much so that some packed it in altogether. Some Teds, gasping in amazement, could not believe what they were witnessing: rockabilly music mixed with New Wave and punk, psychobillies with bleached hair and make-up. With their precious rockabilly hijacked and bastardised, it was simply too much to bear; the movement had

Revival 1972–85

lost its way, wandered too far from the golden path and down a blind alley. Many Teds could not understand what had gone wrong. As one Manchester Ted put it, 'What the fuck are we doing mixing with these weirdoes, we were kicking fuck out of punks all over the country five or six years ago, and here are people on the rocking scene pogoing alongside them!' It also seemed to be the case that quite a few on the rocking scene spent half their time going to northern soul clubs. Many diehard Teds questioned the dedication and commitment of these so called rock and roll fanatics. Others decided to revert back to their original New Edwardian roots, a trend that has become prevalent in the style of today's Teds. It is an introspection and redefinition that is still going on.

Teddy Boys were the first subculture to experience a mass revival. Secondly came the skinheads and then the Mods in the late seventies, all of them traditional enemies of the Teds. Violence increased, with fights with other trendy working-class youths known as 'smoothies' (a term of derision for those who allow themselves to be dictated to by the whims of the fashion/music conglomerates) and also with the Perry Boys or Soul Boys. Many young Teds tried their damnedest to live up to the fearsome reputation their fifties predecessors had acquired. Greasers and Hells Angels were usually friends of the Teddy Boys, mainly down to their shared love of rock and roll and easily traceable common heritage. Still, it was not easy to be a Ted in seventies Britain.

In the fifties, there was only one working-class subculture; by the seventies, there were many rivals. Arch-enemies of the seventies Teds were skinheads (usually into football hooliganism and/or fascist and Nazi politics), gangs of smoothies and gangs of black youths. Most seventies Teds have had more than their fair share of street fights. As a result of the ignorance and even jealousy that the seventies Teds attracted from other

Teddy Boys

youths, flick knives abounded, and there were occasional murders committed by Teds, although these did not cause the moral outrage and panic the fifties Teds sparked in their day. In fairness, it must be said that there were quite a few Teddy Boys in the seventies who were into some far-right movements but this was true of virtually all other working-class subcultures in Britain at that time, and for the Teds at least this did change as time went on. However, the seventies was generally a much more violent decade than the fifties by every indicator and standard.

The fighting often occurred on trips. The Manchester Teddy Boys travelled by coach to rock and roll gigs around the north of England and one such jaunt to Blackpool in 1976 became infamous. The coach parked behind the Pleasure Beach. On disembarking, the Manchester lads met hundreds of Teddy Boys from around the north, some walking along swigging Newcastle Brown Ale from beer bottles and throwing them around, clearly drunk from their own coach journeys. The Teds later converged at the Casino nightclub, where loud rock and roll was being played and where Teddy Boys and their girls jived and bopped outside. A couple of hours later, some Hells Angels and their greaser friends tried to force their way into the Casino without paying. The Teddy Boys inside began to throw pint pots at them, clearing the bar. The Angels retaliated with their belts and some with their crash helmets, but they were overwhelmed. Many were beaten senseless. Some Teds even climbed up onto the roof and set fire to it, and a large table was thrown through the quarter-inch plate glass window of the club. The gig was stopped by the police, with ambulances taking the injured away to hospital and firefighters tackling the blaze on the roof, much to the amusement of the jeering Teds. The police held everybody, but in true Ted solidarity, not a word was said to them. They finally ushered

Revival 1972-85

everybody back onto the coaches and ended the fun, but not for long. The Manchester Teds at the motorway services on the journey back helped themselves to food and drinks and were again ushered back onto the coach and sent on their way.

One of the most famous rivalries of the late seventies was the war between the Teds and the punk rockers. Malcolm McLaren and Vivienne Westwood, two 'entrepreneurs' and wily manipulators of the youth market, owned a boutique called Let it Rock on the Kings Road in west London. It became, as far as the press was concerned, the epicentre of the conflict. In reality the war was fought out in countless skirmishes and battles in cities, towns and estates across the country. Originally selling Ted clothing in 1971 – McLaren himself often sported a drape jacket – but then changing to selling punk and bondage gear in 1976, McLaren and Westwood kickstarted the punk rock subculture with the band the Sex Pistols. McLaren and Westwood must have had a crystal ball and anticipated the Ted–punk street wars that were to be highlighted in all the national newspapers. They apparently knew exactly what they were doing.

The punks adopted and adapted many of the same clothes worn by the Teddy Boys, including ripped and torn off-the-peg drape jackets, scruffy crêpe shoes and bootlace ties. Punk versions were also recorded of classic rock and roll and rockabilly records, most famously when the Pistols, then fronted by Sid Vicious, recorded a couple of Eddie Cochran classics. The punks were also heavily into glue sniffing and drugs. Such perceived disrespect to the New Edwardian style and music was not tolerated by Britain's new generation of young Teds, who felt duty bound to defend the honour of the drape, and the war was on. In truth, it was not a fair fight, with the usually battle-hardened Teds often pulverising the upstart punk rockers.

Teddy Boys

The entire situation was exploited by the press. Is it not a strange coincidence that such clashes between rival sub-cults that take place either in, or within easy drive of, the capital, always seem to be caught on camera by the newspapers when Parliament is in summer recess, the nation is not at war, much of the public is on holiday and there is little or no news? So what if a few thick working-class lads get put in hospital, or even better, are killed? That type of thing sells newspapers! If the truth be known, most of the punks did not view violence as their 'thing', and in later years many original punk rockers sympathised with their former rivals' antipathy to the way the Ted style had been stolen and bastardised by the punks.

Manchester Teds returning from their rock and roll club, the Midland Hotel in West Didsbury, in the mid to late seventies would often converge, eighty to a hundred strong, around the central Piccadilly Gardens area. There they would wait for punks wearing ripped drapes and crêpes and any gear resembling Ted clothing and would beat them senseless with their studded belts, adorned with heavy, lion's head buckles. On one night they chased them into the Ranch Club in Piccadilly, then petrol-bombed the door. The police and fire service arrived and some Teds were arrested, ending up in young offenders' institutions. Many Teds in the seventies had lengthy criminal records, mainly for violence, and did time in detention centres and borstals. It was the same all over the country. They saw themselves, rightly or wrongly, as sticking up for being a Ted, and fighting for the drape.

The levels of violence were at times severe, but within eighteen months the 'war' was over. Some punks ended up switching sides through association with Teds and by getting into their music. Many found they had more in common with each other than they did with the rest of mainstream society. After a few years, the rivalry was forgotten. Many

Revival 1972–85

punks tuned in to the music of the Teds, and some became hepcats/rockabillies or psychobillies, a fact that, as we have seen, had far more serious consequences for the Teddy Boy movement in general.

However, at the time none of this could stop the Ted scene getting bigger and bigger, with rocking clubs opening up all over the country, as demonstrated by the massive Ted march in London in May 1976 that culminated at Picketts Lock. Some Teds who had been teenagers in the late fifties and early sixties began wearing the clothes again. Many of these had older brothers, friends, uncles or fathers who had been Originals in the fifties. These 'tail-end' Teds, who were too young to have been around in the fifties, nevertheless inspired younger people to start wearing the gear and listening to rock and roll. They were a very important group, and tended to form the backbone of the Teds that started the seventies revival. One of them, Boppin' Brian Spilsbury, features in the interviews in this book. There were small pockets of such diehards all over the country.

At the time of the Ted march in London in 1976, numbers peaked and stayed there until around 1980, when the rockabilly movement began to take hold. However, the Teddy Boy movement was always at least twice as big as the rockabilly movement even at the latter's peak, and most rockabillies had been Teds in the seventies anyway. Perhaps a quarter of them were the trendy psychobillies and 'anybillies' who appeared only after 1983.

The seventies failed to see the Teds rid themselves of their thuggish image. Manchester Teds smashed up the city's Free Trade Hall in 1977 and Granada Television refused to screen an early-eighties programme about the Teds, scheduled to be part of a series entitled *Teenage*, directed by Julien Temple and researched by Jon Savage, and featuring Manchester Teddy boys Ray Ferris,

Teddy Boys

Paul Ramsbottom, Sideburn Steve and the boys and girls of the Salford Bop Cats. The reason for Savage, author of the definitive punk rock history *England's Dreaming*, choosing them was because his research had led him back to the original Ted style, and these were the most original Teds he had met, even down to the use of grease on the hair. Upon seeing a photo of Ray Ferris' marriage in 1980, Savage commented, 'This wedding photo looks like it was taken in the nineteen fifties,' due to Ray and his brother Lenny and two other friends, Dave Vincent and Richard Bilton, dressing in original-style drapes that the Salford Bop Cats had been wearing since 1977. Savage was the first notable post-fifties researcher to delve properly into the pre-1955 Teddy Boy style. To Granada TV's shame, the series was never aired, and sits on their shelves to this day. No reasonable explanation for this censorship has ever been given, but the incident stands as a damning testament to the continuing power of the media. Two brilliant articles about this blatant censorship, and about the Ted movement in general, appeared in *The Face* magazine in June 1982.

In the same year, at the Astoria Ballroom in Leeds, the group Clive Osborne and the Clear Notes were gigging, at a time when the rockabilly movement was peaking. The group appeared on stage with dyed blond hair and wearing fifties-style sweaters adorned with musical notes. They began playing trumpets and playing jazz-type rock and roll, in front of 5–600 Teds. The Teds, who had come from across the north of England, did not take long to decide that the group were in fact taking the micky out of the audience. The consequences were inevitable; the Teds rioted. The bouncers on the door were given a severe kicking, as were the bar staff. Hepcats and 'squares' in attendance were flattened by Teddy Boy fists covered in chunky finger rings and feet in crêpe-soled shoes. The Doncaster Rockabillies hurled pint pots, and the

Revival 1972–85

glass main doors were smashed in. The police soon arrived, some on horseback and some in dog vans. The Teds, however, refused to stop rioting for another hour. Eventually things calmed down and the blood was mopped up. Scores were arrested and many Teds still bear the scars from police-dog bites to prove they were there. As one unrepentant Ted put it, 'The band should know their fucking audience. It's like putting a band on from the Ku Klux Klan in front of the Black Power movement.'

The Lakes Hotel, near Belle Vue, Manchester, was for a time a regular haunt of Teddy Boys and it was here in 1984 that a large fight broke out with the Perry Boys, Manchester's particular term for what were known elsewhere as soccer casuals. Perry Boys were in some ways a derivative of the earlier Mods, sporting designer-label clothes, and there was no love lost between them and the Teds of the time. Trouble had been brewing for some weeks, with Rockers' motorbikes being kicked over at another nearby Ted venue, the Gorton Brook, and a classic Ford Consul belonging to a Ted having its windscreen smashed. The Perry Boys had already taken one beating from the Teds for these incidents. The Teds were at the Lakes Hotel to see Ray Ferris's band The Invaders, who had just supported Graham Fenton of Matchbox fame in France. A few Teds came into the hotel and declared that about sixty Perry Boys were on their way over for more aggro. The Teds, around thirty strong, went outside, formed ranks and waited.

They did not have long to wait until the Perries came over a low ridge and advanced on the Teds, throwing bottles and stones and everything they had at the Teds. The Teds stood their ground. The late Dave Willis, six feet three inches tall and resplendent in his grey drapes, jumped the nearby fence and knocked down two Perries, then knocked two more out cold. A general melee of hand-to-hand fighting then ensued, which

Teddy Boys

lasted for around forty-five minutes. The Perry Boys got completely battered and were eventually totally routed. Some Teds had injuries from being hit over the head with planks of wood, but everybody went back into the Lakes Hotel and watched the band, who had also been heavily involved in the fighting. The Perry Boys never returned, and in fact they no longer exist as a coherent group except in the memory of those who were witness to the eighties.

Musically, the seventies Teds are owed a debt of gratitude for, if nothing else, their rediscovery of the long-forgotten sound of rockabilly, a music that, until the Teds found it, had bordered almost on the occult in its obscurity not only in Britain but also in its US homeland. The great revival of the seventies had firmly re-established and cemented the Teddy Boy, however misconceived, in the nation's consciousness. The seventies Teds, like their progenitors of a quarter century earlier, lived life at a furious pace. Burn-out for many was inevitable. But just like the diehard Originals of the fifties, there were some who simply refused to fade away.

There can be no doubt that seventies Ted fashions became more garish and further removed from their original Edwardian inspiration. Bright yellow, red, blue, pink and green drapes were not that uncommon, and velvet on collars, cuffs and pocket flaps was everywhere. Drape jackets became longer and crêpe boppers became ever chunkier, with soles up to two inches thick. And at the same time that the Teddy Boys of the seventies had their own distinctive style, so too did many Teddy Girls, wearing drape jackets, miniskirts and knee-length leather boots. Both the Teds and their girls would have looked anathema if they had dressed like that in the early fifties.

As far as the popular charts were concerned, for the Teds the mid-eighties onwards was generally a musical catastrophe. There were some highpoints, such as when Jackie Wilson's 'Reet Petite'

Revival 1972–85

made the number one spot in the charts in November 1986, and quite a remarkable string of hits for Shakin' Stevens' by now much watered down and very commercial, pop-sounding rock and roll, but by and large that was it.

Many would later say that the influence of glam rock, and the need to stand out in a decade that went colour mad, had turned the original razor-sharp New Edwardian fashion into a clownish parody of itself. But serious introspection usually comes after decline. Metaphorically, this is the time from which the public get their snapshot of the Teds, cementing in their minds but a single frame from an entire film of the history of the Teds. It is a snapshot far removed from the suave and highly original fashion worn by the first New Edwardians a quarter of a century earlier. Time evolved the style, hence the glam-influenced look of the seventies. At the time, however, the Teds loved every minute of it and their style was right for the times they were in. There was no introspection; it was pure existentialism, of the moment, in true Ted disregard for everything but 'the moment'. In this latter cause, and to their immense credit, the seventies Teds were unswervingly true to their fifties roots. It also must be stressed that it was the young Teds of the seventies who firmly established the Teddy Boys as an enduring feature of the British social landscape and not just a passing fad.

In the eyes of many, by the mid-eighties the Teds were finished as a coherent subculture, washed out and dried up. Any that remained were a sad reminder of a best-forgotten, irrelevant past. Of course just as with the Teds of the fifties, many seventies Teds packed it in for good when the scene began to shrink. But ideas are harder to kill than people, and diehard Teds are harder to kill than others may think, or have you believe. Just like the colour of your skin, being a Teddy Boy or girl can't be washed off; it is indelible. And it is the seventies Teds that form the backbone of today's revival movement.

5
Survival 1986–present

There were several reasons for the decline of the Teds from the mid-eighties onwards. In fact all Britain's previous youth subcultures began to decline rapidly as a pervasive, mono-youth culture based upon urban black American rap music and fashion began sweeping the country, actively encouraged by the media and fashion industry. The Ted–rockabilly rivalry had already thinned the number of Teds attending clubs and pubs, most eventually leaving the scene and going 'back into the woodwork'. Many seventies Teds had already disappeared, settling down to have families.

However, nostalgia for the fifties had not disappeared altogether, and 1986 saw the arrival of a popular new series on British TV, *The Russ Abbot Show*. Abbot's Saturday night TV comedy always produced at least one sketch featuring garishly dressed comedy Teds, and these firmly hammered home the image of the loveable, thick-headed, walking fashion disaster that the seventies Teds had come to be perceived as in the mind of the public. The Ted sketches were never cruel, and were usually hilariously funny. Abbot openly revealed his admiration for the Teds and said he was always sad that he had missed out on being a Teddy Boy in his youth. The Teds themselves remember the sketches with fondness, as do the general public, and there was no doubt that they contained an element of truth. The fact is that many of the same sketches could have been made portraying any of the other working-class subcultures and still rung true. But they weren't made about any other subculture,

Teddy Boys

they were made about Teddy Boys. Fame has its price, and that's all there is to it.

In 1993, Dennis Potter's play *Lay Down Your Arms* was turned into a TV series on Channel 4, re-titled *Lipstick On Your Collar*. Set in London during the Suez Crisis, the series was very witty and generally very well received. Many rock and roll hit songs of that year were used, and the fashions were also accurately portrayed.

With the rapid decline of the Teddy Boys, a few remaining diehards began to look back seriously at the roots of their movement with an especially critical eye to fashion detail, and they realised with some amazement, not to say horror, how far the style had become debased from its true Neo-Edwardian origins of the very early fifties. For these diehards, a return to the roots of the 'British genius' was not only well overdue, it was critical to the survival and the future of the British Teddy Boy.

In the nineties, Ritchie Gee, former roadie with Crazy Cavan and the Rhythm Rockers, began organising two weekend gigs a year, one in the summer and one in early December. Known as the Wildest Cats in Town weekenders, these proved to be very popular with remaining Teds in the lean nineties. Today they are attended regularly by about 1,500 people. Similarly, Stuart Hardy promoted two weekend rock and roll festivals per year that were known as the Ted Do and the Valentines Weekender respectively, and these proved just as popular. These weekenders are still taking place today and are busier than ever, with their car parks full of classic American and British automobiles of the fifties, from Ford Zodiacs to '57 Chevrolets and '59 Cadillacs and everything else in between. It must also be stressed that all the old gang rivalries of the past between the various factions and even between individuals of the

Survival 1986–present

movement have long since disappeared and most Teds are on very good terms with each other today.

During the nineties, a new kind of 'rock and roller' began entering the by now, very tame and sedate rock and roll scene. These were couples who although they had been teenagers in the fifties, sixties or seventies, had chosen not to get involved in the Teddy Boy culture that dominated rock and roll venues during those heady decades. Instead they had chosen the conventional lifestyle of 'squares'. By the nineties these people were turning up at the remaining few rock and roll clubs and, having learned to dance 'the rock and roll' in dancing lessons, proceeded to jive all night to jive records. The Teds labelled this group 'jive bunnies', a reference to a series of rock and roll compilation records released in the late eighties and early nineties by the group Jive Bunny and the Mastermixers.

These jive bunnies, now numbering in their thousands, have come to dominate many clubs up and down the country, much to the amazement of the Teds, who, if they bother to turn up at all, watch in bewildered amusement as the dancers, some of whom dress up in garish Ted drapes and circle skirts that look as if they were bought from fancy-dress shops, jive all night to nothing but jiving records, and driving many Teds (who like other forms of rock and roll as well as jive records) away. Many jive bunnies are refugees from the line-dancing craze of the late eighties, and it shows. The jive bunnies are nothing to do with the Teds, and the two groups have almost nothing in common. However there is the argument that the jive bunnies have helped to keep a lot of rock and roll clubs open, especially during the lean years of the nineties. When all is said and done, these people, who are simply rock and roll fans, do nobody any harm and are part of the growing numbers of ordinary people who are fed up with the perceived tyranny of modern 'music'.

Teddy Boys

Through the early years of the new century, more and more Teds began to link up with each other via the internet, at vintage and classic Americana festivals and at reunion weekends. Many had finished rearing children and now found they had time to return to the scene. The Ted Do and the Wildest Cats in Town weekenders continued to help reaffirm the Teddy Boy foundations as a coherent movement and lifestyle. In fashion terms, the return to Edwardian roots has taken a firm hold, but there was also resistance to this trend by some who believe that it was fine to wear whatever you like on the Ted scene so long as everybody was 'rockin'' and that the drive to return to a 'purer' original style was not necessarily a good thing, indeed was an elitist attitude that brought with it the danger of exclusivity. This group denigrate those attempting to return to roots as 'holier than thou, born-again Teds' or worse, and continually call for unity, stating that elitism divides the movement, which will lead to its inevitable fall.

On the other side of the coin, the return-to-roots Edwardians believe that it is necessary to redefine what a Ted is if the movement is to survive with any meaning, and therefore they reject the idea that anyone with a long jacket or who likes rock and roll music can be a Ted, or is a Ted by any other name. To these revisionist Teds, such an attitude displays an ignorance of the movement's history and has continued and will continue, they believe, to result in a scene without any real meaning; if there is nothing to unite around except rock and roll music, this results in just a bland group of music fans no different to any other, and signals the death of the true Teddy Boy spirit. It is an ideological conflict that appears to be irresolvable, as both sides appear to be as passionate about the justness of their cause as each other, and at present there appears to be no common ground between the two schools. A lot of Teds dislike this split and wish it would go away, but it

Survival 1986–present

appears to be a core issue, and hopes of it disappearing seem forlorn. From an outsider's perspective, the whole subject may seem extreme, but then many would argue that true Teds always were extreme.

It is a sad and often embarrassing fact that more than a few people on the scene claim to have been at certain places and events when this was impossible given their age; they were simply too young to have been there. This is a common fault among people who wish to boost their standing and credibility within the movement. However sad this fact is, it is almost inevitable in a subculture that, although it values youth, venerates age and totally rejects modern society's even greater, and more damaging, obsession with attempting to stay forever young. As is seen at gatherings across the country, a few Teds vainly dye their hair in an attempt to look younger. In the eyes of many, this is one of the things that damage the movement. On the other hand most Teds appear to accept old age gracefully when it comes, but never appear to lose that youthful sparkle in their eyes, and never fail to seize the moment. These older Originals look superb with their greying or pure-white hair (or even bald heads!) and always turn up immaculately dressed in razor-sharp Edwardian suits. They are a credit to the movement.

There is a growing interest in alternative lifestyles among today's younger generation who are looking for an alternative to an endlessly repeating, worldwide monoculture. This is reflected in the small yet growing number of youngsters joining today's New Edwardian movement. It is true to state that one of the greatest reasons for the successful recruitment of new people, often young teenagers, into the movement today is that in the unanimous view of the Teds, the world of today, and specifically Britain, is an utter shambles. The Teds appear to offer an equally real and infinitely better

Teddy Boys

alternative. For many Teds, their expressions of despair at the present plight of Britain are unrepeatable, opinions apparently shared by many non-Teds. For many, if not all Teds, the movement itself has now become the Promised Land, and not the politician's consumerist Britain. Perhaps it was always so, but there can be no denying that many of the values held by a lot of today's Teds might initially be considered slightly old fashioned by some of today's teenagers, with one huge exception: the Teds refuse to be pushed around by anyone, and do their own thing regardless of the opinions of others, a value they have held since the very beginning. They have an apparent immunity to criticism aimed at them by those from outside the movement. If they are accused of being closed-minded then the charge cannot be due to ignorance, for every Ted knows full well what the modern world is like, the decision to be a Ted being a deliberate and considered act of will.

This work has taken a year and nearly 2000 hours of research to finalise. It is not possible to thank everyone who has provided help, photographs and information voluntarily, because there are simply too many, and we the authors do not wish to cause offence to anyone by leaving them off some kind of list. Neither is it possible for us to remember everyone we have met, both within the Teddy Boy movement and outside it, who has contributed in some way to our own knowledge, which amounts to a combined total of seventy-two years in the Teddy Boy scene.

In a world that many believe is in a state of continual decline, beset with increasing problems, the twilight of the Originals is well under way. The time will inevitably arrive when the last living member of that elite group, who were once numbered in their hundreds of thousands, will leave this world of

Survival 1986–present

increasing darkness, and the last living link to the trailblazing New Edwardians of the fabulous fifties will be gone forever. All who follow in their wake stand forever in the shadow of their achievement. They were the first, and we shall not see their like again.

> Stand up and be counted, show the world that you're a Ted
> Stand up and prove that rock and roll ain't dead.
> Stand up and fight! Well it's time to bash some heads!
> Stand up and shout, GOD BLESS THE TEDS!

('God Bless The Teds' by the Barnyard Devils, 2010)

Interviews with Teddy Boys (2)

Brian Lewis Stuart, known as 'Rockin' Lewis', aged seventy-one, of Levenshulme, Manchester

The first rockin' place I went to was at Levenshulme skating rink. There was a little café there. In all, I'd say there were about twenty of us in Levenshulme. We were called Teddy Boys; some referred to us as Edwardians. I never carried weapons [but] a couple of them carried knuckledusters and some had flick knives. I never wore belts at first, but later on I did; the studded belts came in with the Rockers in the early 1960s. There were little differences in style, you know, depending on which area you came from.

Yes, there were gang fights. There was a big fight at Belle Vue amusement park with the Liverpool Teds that lasted half an hour. I got arrested for hitting a policeman. The first big fight I remember was in Levenshulme. Yank servicemen from Burtonwood had been trying to pinch our girls. The next week all the Teds came down, and we had belts and knuckledusters, and on Stockport Road we hammered the Yanks. The police cars were everywhere! We used to fight the Moss Side Teds. We fuckin' hammered them. We had Levenshulme, Longsight and Stockport Teds on our side. I knew them all you see, I used to go all over.

I saw my first Teds in '56 with the advent of rock and roll. I got my first drape off Johnny Goodman in '56 when I was fifteen. It was a dogtooth check, black and grey, with no turnback or velvet on the cuff. It had a full three-inch-wide velvet collar and two buttons and a link button. The buttons were

Teddy Boys

cloth-covered and it had flaps on the pockets. The lining was a dark-grey colour. Also it had pants with it; they had fourteen-inch bottoms with a turn-up. There was no waistcoat with it.

My shirt was a cut-away collar type. I often wore a white T-shirt underneath a dark shirt. I had a pair of half-inch-sole crêpes in leather and also a pair of blue suede crêpes. I wore white socks, there were no fancy coloured socks then, and most of my mates wore white socks as well. Some wore the usual waistcoats and watch chains. The girls usually wore two-piece suits in the same colours as the lads. In the late fifties the girls wore US-style circle skirts.

I got my jeans from Greenwoods in Stockport in '57 and you could wear your jeans with your drape. I had a black sports jacket that I wore with slacks or jeans. Winks [winkle-picker shoes] came out in 1960. I never saw any Teds wearing winks in the fifties. All my mates wore crêpes, slip-ons or chukka boots. I wore four rings on each hand. A few wore earrings. Haircuts to start with were just slicked back. Then came the Tony Curtis and the flat top. Some had crew-cuts. I had ear-lobe-length sideburns. There were little differences in styles from one area to another. I noticed these when I used to go up to Blackburn and Colne. I never saw anyone drink-drive. Not many had cars.

Pianos were played by Teds in a lot of the pubs, usually rock and roll and boogie-woogie. A Ted nicknamed 'Tarzan' used to play the piano.

There was a lot more velvet as years went by. To start with there was no velvet at all, then it was on collars, just the back of the collar. About 1959, when I was working down Bradford Colliery, I saw roll collars in velvet. I never saw any red or yellow drapes. There was dogtooth, windowpane check in powder blue, greys, blacks and browns. I saw Scottish Teds in the fifties, some of them wearing Scottish sashes. I had blue-

Interviews with Teddy Boys (2)

black and red-black cheese-cutter hats, but I only wore them if it was raining. I never saw Teds wearing long chains with keys on the end. Most drapes had two or three buttons with a link button; I can't remember there being any with four buttons. My mate Spider had a black, calf-length drape and tight pants with twelve-inch bottoms, but he was eccentric.

The Teds started dying off in about 1962. I carried it on in the sixties with a few others: Bobby Needham, Boppin' Brian, Yank, Smokey, Kenny Doyle and seven or eight others kept going right through the sixties. In the sixties, the Originals kept fifties rock and roll alive. It was hard to find places to go that did rock and roll then.

I did a programme for Granada [Television] on the Teds in the early seventies. We were stood outside the Railway pub in Levenshulme, and a bloke from Granada TV pulled up in his car and said, 'Blimey, I don't believe this, Teddy Boys in the seventies! We've got to do a programme on this.' We got paid for it. We said, 'We love rock and roll, and that's it!' We told him we got our drapes made at Jacksons on Stockport Road.

When we did the Granada programme, it all started again at the same time, 1972. The Mid [Midland Hotel] started in 1972. We were asked to do another programme on dancing. We showed how we jived. Granada provided the girls but they didn't wear the right gear. We said, 'What the bleedin' hell is this?' They sent them back to get the right gear on. Then we bopped. It was all filmed. I was thirty-two. There were only a few 'Originals' left by then. A lot were new generation whose dads were Teds. We started going to the Mid and it was packed right through the seventies. In the seventies I had a powder-blue drape, a maroon drape and a black drape. I also had waistcoats. The half-moon pockets were really a seventies thing. I went down to the Black Raven pub in London in 1973 with about six or eight of us and I met

Teddy Boys

'Sunglasses Ron' [the self-proclaimed 'King of the Teds', Ron Staples] there. Ron spotted that we were from Manchester by the way that we jived.

In the seventies, the style went ridiculous. Bands like Showaddywaddy made us Teds look like bloody fools. I must make a point. When the rockabillies came out at the start of the eighties, a lot of Teds stopped going. The rockabilly movement ruined the Ted scene.

I still love rock and roll. The Teds to me, I'll tell you what I think: the Teds are a legend, a legend in our times.

Interviews with Teddy Boys (2)

Dennis Burnier Smith, aged sixty-five, of Broughton, Salford. Dennis lived in Newton Heath, Manchester, when he was a boy

I was about ten when I saw my first Teddy Boys. It was during the Whit Walks on Oldham Road in Manchester. That would be around 1956. There were two of them, and I remember that it was then that I wanted to be a Teddy Boy. They were cool and had swagger. My dad said, 'I don't know where they get the money from to buy their £25 suits.' In those days £25 was the equivalent of three weeks' wages. But I remember hearing about them [Teddy Boys] in 1954.

I have had loads of drapes and all sorts of waistcoats. I got my first drape when I was about thirteen, in '58 or '59. It was royal blue with two flap pockets at the top and two at each side. It had a ticket pocket on the left. The width of the collar was two inches and the pocket flaps were one inch wide. It had no cuffs. It was finger-tip length, all my drapes were finger-tip length. My trousers were high-waist with thirteen-and-a-half-inch width at the bottom, with one-inch turn-ups, but I was a young lad with skinny legs. I remember that, as I ordered them often. I used to wear my trousers with a belt with a smallish buckle. I got sent home from school a few times for wearing drainpipe trousers.

I wore ordinary white shirts with a pin collar. My ties were all Slim Jim style worn in a Windsor knot and held with a stud pin. I didn't see anyone wearing a bootlace tie in the fifties, I only wore one in 1964–5. We all wore Slim Jims. Some did wear cravats but they were not my style. Some Teds would wear a pastel-coloured, V-necked sweater over their shirts.

I wore crêpes with one-and-a-half-inch-thick soles at the heel, with the rest of the sole being about one-inch thick. The uppers were 'castle tops': tooled leather with a fancy intricate

Teddy Boys

pattern on them. I saw Teds wearing chukka boots and brogue-style shoes. Some wore slip-ons but I didn't; not my style. I wore chukka boots myself from about 1959–61. I also used to wear Chelsea boots with a Cuban heel. I got them from a shop called Bata on Oldham Street in Manchester. I wore winkle-pickers in the early sixties; they came out in 1959–60 with the Italian suits. I always wore white socks. I never saw any Teds wearing fluorescent socks, ever. I remember 'ratter' [cheese-cutter] hats on Teds but I never wore one.

I always ordered a bright-red lining on all my waistcoats. Some of my waistcoats had roll collars and some didn't. The roll collar influence came from the US jazz-blues singers. My brightest drape was royal blue with a raindrop fleck pattern on it. I never saw any red drapes about in the fifties. There were a lot of dogtooth drapes about. All my drapes had four buttons at the front and a link button. Not many had more than just velvet on the collars. I saw mostly black velvet and also dark blue; I only saw light-grey velvet on grey suits. I got married in 1965 wearing a drape, and that was a four-button drape. It had busman's cuffs on it, where the piping runs up the arm and comes together to form a point [and] had three buttons on each cuff. I had a mate who used to wear a drape made out of doeskin, with half-moon pockets. I remember Teds wearing Prince of Wales check drapes. I used to get all my drapes made by John Temples in Leeds because they could make any style you could think of.

Not many Teds wore overcoats. Some wore Crombies with velvet collars. I never wore watch chains but some of my mates did. I carried a flick-knife for years, but I should say I never used it. My mate used to carry a knuckleduster and he never used that either. I knew Jimmy Monaghan, alias 'Swordsy' [a very tough Manchester boxer who fought under the name Jim Swords in the sixties]. He had a big

Interviews with Teddy Boys (2)

crew of Teds in Miles Platting. [But] I never saw any gang fights between Teds.

I used to wear sideburns, I'd say they were about ear-lobe length. Most wore them like that but I did have a mate who wore them longer than that, right down to where they met his jaw. The longer sideburns really came in more in the sixties. I used to have a 'Southbank' hair style; it came in about '56. The early Teds just used to wear their hair greased straight back. I used to blow my hair in over the gas stove. A lot used to wear flat tops with the hair long at the sides and greased back. I used to use Vaseline or Brylcreem. Of course the Tony Curtis haircut, he was the one that started the style with the quiff.

The girls used to wear pedal pushers or pumps or flat shoes, for jiving in. They [also] used to wear like a bolero jacket and flared skirts. Their hair was mainly the ponytail style. Beehives came in about '59–60.

Early on I liked Jerry Lee Lewis, Elvis and Buddy Holly, but my idol was Gene Vincent. I liked skiffle, but most of my collection was US rhythm and blues. We couldn't get hold of any US singles in the fifties, the nearest we had here was Billy Fury, not Cliff [Richard], oh no. Billy Fury was the man.

A lot of the Teds got drafted into the Forces when they were eighteen years old. I didn't see any black lads in the Teds, but I knew a couple of Caribbean lads, and they stayed with their own style, but we all got on pretty well together.

I became a Rocker in the sixties. The Teds and Rockers were very closely allied. I finally stopped wearing my drape around 1971, when I was twenty-five.

The Teddy Boys, the music, it was great, the style was great, and for the first time we had money. We were an elite. I think it is one of the smartest styles around, ever. I think it's a great thing that you are keeping it going. Really great.

Teddy Boys

'Boppin' Brian Spilsbury, aged sixty-four

When I was eight years old, I heard people talking about them [the Teds], that would be about 1956. I saw a lot of Teds around Belle Vue [in Manchester]. There was a lot in the papers about them. In 1958, when I was eleven, my best mate, Dave Evans, worked in Raffo's Café, and I got to know a lot of Teds in there, and that's when I decided I wanted to be a Ted. I am what you'd call a second-generation Ted; I was too young to be a proper fifties Ted. My auntie took my trousers in for me and I started combing my hair into a DA hairstyle. My mum bought me a pair of crêpes with one-inch-thick soles, and I remember they cost thirty-nine shillings and eleven pence. When I was thirteen, I was what I would call a semi-Ted. I used to wear my dad's jacket to make it look as if I was wearing a drape jacket. The music I was into was Gene Vincent, Buddy Holly and Eddy Cochran.

From about 1958, when I moved to secondary modern school, the headmaster used to come round during assembly like he was in the Army and inspect everybody. Anybody with tight trousers or anything that looked like a Ted haircut or any creeper shoes would be ordered out of the line and sent to his office to receive punishment with the strap and told that dressing like that you would be classed as 'one of them' [a Teddy Boy]. This would happen every morning without fail, but us Teds didn't care and just carried on getting the strap. The headmaster got his comeuppance in the end though, because one day Alan Tottoh, who became a very well-known boxer in the sixties after he had left school, came back and punched the headmaster.

I remember going to the cinema in the fifties with my mum and dad, and there was this little gang of Teds walking around, and my dad said, 'Who the hell do they think they are?' You

Interviews with Teddy Boys (2)

always got older men in the streets commenting, 'If they were in the Army with me, I'd soon sort them out,' meaning the Teds. But we were not all hooligans. A lot of Teds in the fifties were only in it because it was the 'in' thing. They were fickle. Only a few stuck with it when the fashions changed. I think National Service killed a lot of it off, but not all of it. A lot of Teds went straight back into it when they had done their National Service. I know Teds who would not hurt a fly. My mate Johnny Goodwin went into the Army in 1956, came out in '58 and went straight back into the Teds. Most of the Teds went in and did their National Service, fought in Suez, Malaya, etc. without moaning at all. People forget this, but it is very important. Plenty of Teddy Boys died for this country. I was in the TA from late 1972 until '74. There was one Ted I knew who was deaf and dumb. He was obviously not in it for the music but simply to be a Ted. It pisses me off that people think it is all about the music, it is not. It's about much more than that.

In 1962, I left school and got my first job, it was in engineering, and then bought my first drape. I was only fifteen, so my dad had to sign the papers for me because I was paying weekly for it. Then I bought a secondhand drape. It was black with four buttons on it and a three-inch-wide collar. No, it had no velvet or cuffs on it. My first drape was fingertip length navy blue with a half velvet collar. It had two breast pockets and two side pockets but no ticket pockets [and] black round velvet cuffs. I used to get my drapes made over in Yorkshire, at John Temples in Leeds. My trousers were fourteen-inch bottoms with turn-ups and my socks were white or sometimes mustard yellow. I never saw any fluorescent socks in the fifties or the sixties. Most Teds I knew wore their sideburns to earlobe length but in the late fifties they got slightly longer. In the sixties, especially in London, you had long-haired Teds

Teddy Boys

with long sideburns, but long hair and long sideburns were generally in fashion then anyway.

I remember Teds wearing normal black shoes or leather brothel creepers in the fifties. Some Teds did wear stovepipe trousers and waistcoats, and I think this was probably influenced by US Westerns and some borrowing from the Beau Brummel look. I never saw any bright drapes. There were lots of greys, blacks and blue drapes, but no green. I saw two or three lads with Mohican hair cuts in the late fifties but I don't know if they were Teds or not.

By 1963–4, when fashions began to change, I was still wearing my drapes and listening to rock and roll records. People asked when I was going to change and I used to reply, 'Never!' and they just all accepted it. Some of the Rockers wore crêpes and ice-blue jeans with their leather jackets. They also wore studded belts for fighting with. Some of them even wore drapes to go out in. The early Rockers were all into rock and roll like Johnny Kidd and the Pirates. The original Teds seemed to have disappeared by '63–4, so I thought I was on my own. My best mate at the time, Dave Evans, stuck with it until '64, then he got married. However, I knew that the Teds were still around because I used to read the *Record Mirror* which catered for the rock and roll fans, and I used to read the letters from London Teds who used to slag off the modern music. In about '65 I was in the cellar of a shop in Cheetham Hill, looking through old records, when I saw a copy of Webb Pierce's 'Teenage Boogie', a classic, yet very obscure at that time, rockabilly record on the Brunswick label, worth now around £1,000. All the Teds in the sixties had big record collections, rare Sun records, we dug out as much rare rockabilly as we could find. We started everyone off on it. We got auction lists and found all sorts of ways of outdoing each other.

Interviews with Teddy Boys (2)

Yes, I used to carry weapons. I began when I was fourteen, carrying a bicycle chain. In the sixties I had a pair of brass knuckledusters. In 1960–61 I wore a studded belt, but only with my jeans because it was a bit scruffy. Between 1960–62 I wore an army webbing belt with metal studs in. At the end of the sixties I used to carry a flick knife. A lot of Teds used to carry a length of rubber hose with a steel rod inside that was about a foot long. I used my bike chain in a fight one time. I have seen all these weapons used in fights. At the 'Rink', a skating rink [on Birchfield Road between Longsight and Levenshulme, south Manchester] that doubled as a dance hall at night, they used to search us before we went in. One night I saw a big table covered in confiscated weapons. It later became a night club in the seventies and was called Ocean's Eleven. All these places, the dance halls, have gone now, it's all night clubs. There were always fights at the Rink. The Moss Side Teds used to come over for fights.

Raffo's was for Teds in the fifties, and in the sixties it became a Rockers' place, so I used to go there. My dad warned me not to go there because it got a bad reputation in the fifties. Before the Mod era of the sixties, we used to go out to dance, for socialising and for the music. There was none of this binge drinking and girls scrapping [that] you get today. It's a different world now, a much worse world. The music is shit and the fashions are shit. To me if you want to hear modern music, just keep repeating the words 'bum-shit bum-shit' over and over and you've got it. I can't believe so many people today dance to bum-shit. They are like sheep, dancing to sheep-shit cheap-shit as well, ha ha. It's all gone to pot. In the sixties it was more peaceable, nobody ever challenged me, and I wanted to know people. I was friendly.

In late '65 I met a postman named Malcolm Breeley in a record shop. He was wearing his postman's uniform but

Teddy Boys

had a quiff in, sideburns and was wearing brothel creepers. Then in '66 I met 'Smokey' [real name Jed Davidson], who was an Original and still wearing the gear and we became mates. That was in Brown's School of Dancing on Stockport Road in Levenshulme. The next night I met Rockin' Lewis [Brian Lewis Stuart]. He was wearing his drape, and bought me a pint, and so then there were three Teds in Levenshulme. Later I met Kenny Doyle, Bob Needham [now deceased], and Yank [now deceased], and then Lewis' brother Colin. There were about five of us Teds that I knew who stuck it right throughout the sixties.

In 1964 I went to the Hollywood youth club, where I met half a dozen Teds all wearing black drapes. This was in Stockport, just off Mersey Square, and they absolutely hated the Mods and all the changes going on.

It all began to take off again after we did a programme for Granada Television. In 1972, the Midland Hotel in West Didsbury opened up with rock and roll on Saturday nights. The resident band was the Rocking One Percent. To start with there were only a few Teds there, but by '73 it was jam-packed with Teds and they came from all over, even the London Teds used to come up. I wore my drapes all through the seventies, but it became a lot more violent, due mostly to squares taking the piss and then them getting a good smacking. The seventies was a fantastic time for the Teds, and we also got hold of all the old obscure rock and roll and rockabilly records that you couldn't get, or had never even heard of, in the fifties. It was the Teddy Boys who rediscovered rockabilly when the rest of the world did not even know what it was. The style got ridiculous though, with a lot of Showaddywaddy, bright-coloured drapes.

After we had done the programme about the Teds for Granada TV, in March 1971, I was in the Wheatsheaf pub

Interviews with Teddy Boys (2)

in Levenshulme with four or five other Teds when a gang of skinheads, about a dozen strong, came in and asked if they could come into our pub. They said they had seen us on the telly and their parents had told them, 'You will never beat that lot.'

I never saw a Ted wearing winkle-pickers until the seventies. Until the seventies, only the beat boys wore them with the Italian look. In fact I never saw Teds wearing suede crêpes until the seventies. Before then, crêpes were always leather and we used to polish them until they were really shiny. We used to bull them up. I used to wear white shirts. I got my first bootlace tie in 1962. I also used to make my own ties. I never saw lads in the fifties wearing velvet collars, or any velvet at all, but it was mentioned in the media.

By the mid-eighties, the Ted scene was dead. You were getting a lot of pretend Teds [jive bunnies], so I went into the woodwork. There was simply nowhere to go. Then in 2010 the Manchester Teds got going again and I joined them. They are Teds recreating the original, pre-rock and roll Ted style.

The Teds have had an absolutely massive impact. I've always been proud to be a Ted and be different from everyone else. It is the best thing to be in, and the fifties is the best thing since sliced bread. I have always been a Ted. It's in my heart.

Teddy Boys

John van Rheede Toas, known as 'Nidge', originally of Horsforth near Leeds

There was no obvious reason or direct influence why I decided to become a Teddy Boy. Although I was born right in the middle of the rock and roll era, in May 1957, my parents were never rock and rollers or Teds; in fact they would have been considered totally square. I remember as a small boy that my parents and grandparents referred to Teddy Boys as 'ruffians' and 'juvenile delinquents' and our family were as far removed from them as anyone could be.

My father had served in the British Army in colonial Kenya right at the end of the Second World War. On coming over to England he had met my mother, a dyed-in-the-wool, Yeadon-born, Yorkshirewoman from Rawdon, at a dance at Broadway Hall, Horsforth near Leeds in the late 1940s. Both families were very traditional. My father's parents were staunch Church of England and my mother's were Methodists. After leaving the Army, my father returned to his accountancy career and in his spare time he was a scout master. Due to being an accountant, my father was able to work in a multitude of different industries, however living in the West Riding of Yorkshire he worked in the dying and finishing trade for a number of years. This was where he gained his knowledge about cloth for suitings. It was traditional at the time for men, especially white-collar workers, to have their suits tailored. I remember often accompanying my father to Davidson's Tailors in Leeds for his suit fittings. This is where one of the influences of my later tailor-made Teddy Boy suits may have come from.

My mother had worked as a wages clerk during the Second World War at the Avro factory at Yeadon Aerodrome, which manufactured Lancaster bomber aircraft for the Royal Air Force. She later worked in other secretarial jobs, prior to my

Interviews with Teddy Boys (2)

arrival in May 1957. She was a choral singer in the Methodist church and her tastes in music were Handel and Mozart, definitely not rock and roll. After I was born, my mother never went out to work again. She was the traditional Yorkshire housewife who stayed at home to bring up the children and work hard, undertaking all the household chores, which was the order of things during the 1950s and early 1960s.

My first memory of coming across Teddy Boys was in the twilight years of their first heyday, when I went on a family trip to Blackpool, Lancashire, in the late summer of 1961, at the age of four years. We travelled to Blackpool with friends of my parents called Jack and Renie Footitt in their Morris Minor Traveller car to see the Illuminations. I clearly remember seeing Teddy Boys walking in groups along the promenade, wearing drape jackets and kiss-me-quick cowboy hats. I also remember leather-jacketed Rockers wearing these hats. These images have always stuck in my mind and were to have a major psychological impact on me later in life. This was interestingly at a point in youth culture when Teddy Boys had largely died out in terms of fashion in Britain.

In my view, the re-emergence of the Teddy Boy really came from a spin-off from the Rockers and Greasers, backed by the so-called rock and roll revival that started in 1967. When I first went to secondary school in 1968, there were a number of Rockers and Greasers, who were in the third and fourth years and wore studded black leather jackets, complete with black drainpipe jeans with red or yellow piping, turned-up bottoms and creepers, colloquially known as beetle crushers. These lads unknowingly had a major influence on me, however at the time, being a straitlaced eleven-year-old, I could not have imagined that I would want to model myself on them only a few years later.

By the age of fifteen, I had decided to stay on into the fifth

Teddy Boys

year to do CSE and GCE 'O' levels. At this same time, a friend of mine from junior, Tony Metcalfe, had left his secondary school at fifteen and had started work at a local clothing manufacturers in Horsforth. Tony used to pass our house prior to me going to school every morning and after I had got home from school. However, it wasn't the fact that Tony was an old friend that made me notice him, it was the fact that he had adopted the Teddy Boy look. Tony wore a black suit, although not a drape, and sometimes a black leather jacket with a white shirt and black suede creepers. Wow, I thought, this is how I want to look! I decided that this was the image that I would like to adopt as it was totally different from the run-of-the-mill image that everyone had adopted. At that time, 1971–2, young working-class teenagers at my school were sporting the suedehead, bootboy and later the 'smoothie' image, which I hated. I started to grow my hair and style it into a quiff with a duck's arse, and when I needed a new pair of shoes, I convinced my mother to allow me to go into Leeds and purchase a brand new pair of Stylo castletop creepers.

The American comedy rock and roll revival band Sha Na Na had quite an influence on me. They were first seen at the 1968–9 Woodstock festival. The sixties band the Dave Clark Five produced the *Good Old Rock 'n' Roll* EP in 1969 and I remember going into a local transport café especially to listen to this and pose in either my leather or drape during my early Ted years. The 1972 London Rock and Roll Show had a major influence on increasing the ranks of the seventies Teds, however the traditional artists like Bill Haley, Jerry Lee Lewis, Little Richard and Chuck Berry eventually gave way to the music that dominated the Ted scene of the seventies, namely rockabilly. Then rockabilly artists such as Carl Perkins, Johnny Burnette and Charlie Feathers came to the fore, along with otherwise unknown American artists in Britain like

Interviews with Teddy Boys (2)

Warren Smith, Sleepy LaBeef and Hank Mizell. Homegrown favourites like Crazy Cavan became the idols of the seventies Teddy Boy scene and developed their own sound known as crazy rhythm, which was a form of rockabilly. Other bands, such as the original Shakin' Stevens and the Sunsets and the Riot Rockers, became very big.

The Ted scene was originally much stronger in nearby Bradford than Leeds and you could always get rock and roll gear in Bradford. We all bought our George Cox creepers at Industrial Trades Footwear on Thornton Road. In those days the creepers were a one-inch crêpe wedge and no more. I remember old Leo in his brown shop-coat who ran the shop and originally came from Peckham in South London, he could always put you right regarding George Cox creepers. The first rock'n'roll pub I went into in Leeds was the Wybeck Arms with my local Ted mate Jimmy Fletcher. We used to go there on Sunday nights on my Honda CB250 G5 and this is where we met up for what was to become a long association with these newly found mates: well-known Leeds Teds like Big Jerry Townes, Brian and Dave Johnson, Dennis Peace, Wolf, Dave 'Melbourne' Williamson, Henry Karasiewicz, Nick Kovrija, Terry Best, Ian, Della, the late Rory and FA, Martin Gravill, Mick and Eric Fisher, Adrian Clayton, Dave 'Bambi' Bainbridge, Neil and Dave Flaxman to name but a few.

We used to get into scrapes and fights all the time in those days and we did not think anything of it, as it was all part of being a Teddy Boy in the seventies and early eighties.

I used to attend 'Jock's Rock and Roll Hop' at Woodhouse Moor Workingmen's Club in Leeds on a Thursday evening. One night there was a big fight with some locals who were much bigger and older than most of us and I got a real hiding from a much older guy and ended up in a crumpled lump at the bottom of the stairs. Once I had washed the blood off and combed my quiff back in, I got back upstairs and carried on boppin' and the guy was banned from the club.

On another occasion the Leeds Teds and some of the Wakefield Teds were on a night out in Huddersfield and while we were in a pub, a local started on a mate of mine called Stevie B and the whole pub erupted. Steve had all on to put him down, so I joined in and kept punching this guy but he would not go down, so I got hold of a chair and used that on him. Someone then said, 'The law are coming,' so I made a cool, sharp exit and went to stop in a mate's pub in Wakefield that night.

On another occasion, in the early 1980s, I was not so successful at evading the strong arm of the law and got arrested in Ossett, a small Yorkshire market town between Wakefield and Dewsbury. The irony was that on this occasion we were not even scrapping with anyone. I arrived in Ossett with a group of Leeds Teds for a rock 'n' roll night at the Town Hall. As was, and still is, the tradition of the Leeds Teds, we decided to go on a pub crawl prior to going to 'the do'. Obviously the West Yorkshire Police were prepared for trouble and had deployed constables at strategic points around the town, mainly outside pubs. We had hardly got any real ale down our necks when we came across two PCs waiting outside a pub. For some reason they did not want us to go in the pub, so we had a bit of an argument with them and called them fascists. Well they did not like that and told us to move on or they would arrest us. As we moved away from them, my friend Tony Hennigan and I shouted abuse, with phrases like 'PC Plod, yeah you are the fascist Plods!' Well that was it; Tony and I were immediately arrested and put in the back of a Black Maria. I complained at being arrested and, with both hands handcuffed behind my back, I promptly received a number of punches to my face, causing blood to ruin one of my light-coloured drapes. Tony and I got slung in the cells. I remember my then-girlfriend,

Interviews with Teddy Boys (2)

Tracy Cox, came to visit us with the rest of the Leeds Teds. We got out the next morning and found a train back to Leeds.

A few weeks later, we were bailed to appear before Wakefield Magistrates Court on charges of being drunk and disorderly. The funny thing is, I decided to conduct my own defence after watching loads of trials on TV; I always fancied myself as a barrack-room lawyer. I remember pleading not guilty and interviewing both the PC who arrested me and a number of Teds, including my girlfriend, Tracy, and another Teddy Girl, Tricia Cox. I asked the PC how could he tell the difference between someone who was drunk and someone who was tired. Well despite me telling the bench that we were respectable Teddy Boys and Girls and law-abiding citizens, and that I had an Army background as an NCO and was currently serving as a Territorial Army NCO, we were fined £25 each and bound over to keep the peace.

As far as the clothing was concerned, I remember a number of peculiarities. There was a particular style that came from the Rockers and this was for black drainpipe jeans with red or yellow piping with turned-up bottoms. These seemed to disappear towards the late seventies. Many Teds, including me, wore these with drapes as well as leathers. I was also a biker, and could be seen not only in leathers but riding a Triumph Trident 160V in a drape on a night out. It is true that the seventies drapes were much louder than the original drapes worn in the fifties and the early sixties. I wore drapes (trimmed with black velvet) in maroon, black, ice blue, royal blue, scarlet red and finally, as I matured, in grey pinstripe. There was a fad for black drapes with red velvet, the same type as you see on the front cover of the seventies LP *Rock 'n' Roll is Still Alive*, but I refused to wear this style, as I thought it was not authentic. What I wore was probably not that authentic, but it was to me at the time.

Teddy Boys

I tended to model myself on Ringo Starr as he appeared in the 1973 film *That'll be the Day*, and some of the Bradford Teds and those I had seen working on the fairgrounds who were ex-Rockers, as I then thought that they looked the most authentic, with their hair Brylcreemed rather than lacquered. Eventually I chose lacquer instead of Brylcreem. We always wanted to sport the best quiff.

I was always a diehard Ted and I still am. I hated the plastic Teddy Boys, who were really smoothies who just wanted to wear a drape and pretend to be a Ted. I would occasionally go up to these guys and knock some sense into them, although I am not a violent person by nature. These were influenced by bands like Showaddywaddy and Les Gray's Mud. We Teds despised the fashions of both bands.

As Leeds Teds, we would always meet on Friday nights in the Viaduct Pub in Lower Briggate and on Saturday lunchtimes. At this time we would either go to other towns and see groups or go to the East Ward Conservative Club at Cross Green in Leeds and then on to the Gaiety Club in Harehills. On a Monday night, we all went to the Fforde Greene pub in Harehills where we saw all the top bands such as Cavan, Shakin' Stevens and the Sunsets, Little Tina and Flight 56, Billy Fury, Sleepy LaBeef, Graham Fenton's Matchbox, local bands Namesake and Hot Foot Gale, to name but a few.

As the seventies became the eighties, there emerged the hepcats, who evolved from some of us Teds, with their box jackets and flat-top hair styles. We, the diehard Leeds Teds, had a few skirmishes with these hepcats during the early eighties, however we had to accommodate these within the rock and roll scene as the numbers of Teddy Boys had started to dwindle during the early eighties. I used to run the disco at the Whip Pub in Leeds on Friday and Saturday nights for a good while. 'Jock' always ran the rock and roll disco at the

Interviews with Teddy Boys (2)

nearby Mucky Duck, or White Swan, and we always ended up in there. These were some of the roughest pubs that you could imagine, but we loved them. Eventually I only did Fridays at the Whip because I missed the trips with the Teds to other nearby towns to go to see bands.

I should point out something quite significant amongst the movement that occurred in the mid eighties. A group of younger Teds in Farnborough, Hampshire, led by Paul Culshaw, decided to adopt and recreate the original pre-1955 Edwardian image. These Teddy Boys, which also included Jerry Lunn, Richard Wooley and Frankie Calland, went a long way to reclaiming the original style that had become diluted. They were some of the first in the early eighties to reject the seventies glam-rock-influenced image and adopt the original Edwardian, pre-1955 style to excellent effect.

According to Jerry Lunn, one of the main influences in adopting the authentic Edwardian style were pictures from old copies of *Picture Post* magazine, along with other similar press cuttings from the early to mid-fifties and the occasional correct image gleaned from books with pictures of 1950s Edwardians such as Colin Donellan and Alex Cruickshank. Paul Culshaw, however, was really the first member of the group to adopt this early authentic style and he was influenced by photographs from *Picture Post* and the like. Another of the old gang, Steve Ferrin, had found photos of his dad who had been a Teddy Boy back in the fifties, and the pictures were of this earlier style.

About the same time, in 1985, I got a mature-student grant to attend a college in Worcestershire to undertake a diploma course. After that I moved to York for a while, and by 1988 I had got married in Zimbabwe and that is when I slowly drifted away from the Teddy Boy scene in England. I did get married in a white drape with white George Cox creepers

Teddy Boys

in Bulawayo in Zimbabwe and this did cause a bit of a stir amongst the old British expats who had gone to Rhodesia in the late fifties to early sixties. My wife, Roseanne, and I then went to live in Malawi, Zimbabwe and South Africa for a few years. By then there were kids and the story is then the same as for many other people. During my time in Africa there was no Ted scene, however I did not change my style and my love of the music. Many Africans were able to walk by our house in Lilongwe, Malawi and hear the sounds of Johnny Burnette blaring out of the window.

Most of my drapes I gave away to Malawian Africans during the early nineties, mainly due to the fact that they did not fit me anymore, so there are probably a few Bush Africans wearing my drapes to this day. The Malawians really haven't a clue what the suits really represented, although I did try to explain to them about Teddy Boy culture in England. I suppose that from an African point of view, they were just brightly coloured, smart, tailored suits that they could dress up to go to church in on Sundays.

While I was out in Africa during the nineties, the Teds continued but by now in lower numbers. The Weymouth, Great Yarmouth and, later, Skegness Ted weekenders took place and this started to set the scene for a more national Ted movement. Weekenders were nothing new, but I think the Hemsby weekenders that started in the seventies and were initially dominated by the Teds and Crazy Cavan had been hijacked, and Hemsby became dominated by the hepcats. I think another, literal death blow to the Ted movement was the death of Ron Staples, the widely acclaimed 'King of the Teds', or to give him his correct name, Ron Fahey. On 22 May 1997, with great sadness, 'Sunglasses' Ron was laid to rest at Edmonton Crematorium, following his death ten days previous after a long battle against cancer, at the tender age of fifty-three.

Interviews with Teddy Boys (2)

Due to the fact that I left England in 1989–90, I missed out on the formation of The Edwardian Drape Society (TEDS) and the initial years of the move towards reclaiming the original Edwardian style of dress. I have to say though that to some degree we had all started to become more conservative in our form of dress as the eighties advanced. In 1984, I had my first grey pinstripe three-piece drape with black velvet trimmings and my trademark half-back collar made up by Keith Wilson in Lower Briggate, Leeds. This pre-dated the formation of TEDS by approximately ten years. All the same, I think that as we got older we would have largely adopted a more conservative style of Teddy Boy dress as a matter of course. At the time of its formation, The Edwardian Drape Society was considered by many Teds as elitist and responsible for splitting up the scene. Nevertheless, I do believe that the formation of the Society and its ideals have been largely responsible for saving the movement from fading into insignificance in this country.

The Edwardian Drape Society came about due to a number of factors. It started largely because in the early nineties, many mainstream Teddy Boys felt that a return to the more authentic original styles was overdue. Many considered that the scene had lost direction. Numbers had drastically dwindled, with many either giving up the scene or defecting to the hepcats or rockabillies. During the seventies and eighties, the 'glam' image had infiltrated the scene, and the original style had become diluted and, to a large degree, lost.

The idea of a more conservative 'Edwardian' style of dress was initially spearheaded by two sisters, Dixie and Suzie, and by Ritchie Gee, who ran the Tennessee Club in Tottenham, Middlesex. The Edwardian Drape Society was formed during 1993–4 to reclaim and perpetuate the original 1950s style.

Teddy Boys

There has since been a move amongst mainstream Teddy Boys in the UK to return to this original image. In general this has now been largely achieved and most Teddy Boys and Girls are now wearing a more authentic 1950s form of dress. However, like all of these things, I think some controversy and snobbery has occurred and continues because of this. One of the main issues has been the use of the term 'Edwardian' as opposed to that of simply 'Teddy Boy', which has caused some disagreement. Another has been the disdain by the 'New Edwardians' towards the few Teds who wish to hang on to their more flamboyant seventies attire, including the wearing of very thick-soled creepers as opposed to the wearing of Oxfords or chukka boots.

In my view, we need to go back to that period during 1953, after a *Daily Express* newspaper headline shortened Edward to Teddy and coined the term 'Teddy Boy'. In my view the terms New Edwardian and Teddy Boy are one and the same thing. The only difference is that the majority who have adopted the more conservative style call this the Edwardian style as opposed to Teddy Boy. I have to say that I now consider myself to be an Edwardian Teddy, as opposed to simply an Edwardian, although I wear a more conservative Edwardian style these days. In saying this, I have every respect for the few Teds who still wear the seventies gear; however, I think the reason that I have adopted the more conservative form of dress is because I am older and more conventional in my outlook these days.

Sometime after returning to the UK from Africa, I started to get back into contact with my old Teddy Boy mates up in Leeds and slowly started to re-acquire the gear. I firstly contacted Dave 'Melbourne' Williamson after seeing his York rock and roll website. Dave runs all the rock and roll events up at the Leeds Irish Centre and other venues around the Leeds and York area. The first thing he asked me after getting

Interviews with Teddy Boys (2)

over the shock of hearing a voice from around twenty-five years previous was, 'Have you still got your quiff?' to which I replied, 'Yes.' He replied, 'You bastard, I've lost mine!' I then went up to Leeds to attend the next Irish Centre event and met up with people that I hadn't seen for years. Some had changed beyond all recognition and yet for some the years had been kind and they had not changed a bit. Most people remarked that I hadn't changed at all, which was flattering, however I am older, my hair isn't quite as thick as it was and I have put on the customary weight of middle age, despite re-engaging into the Territorial Army in 1996.

This getting back on the Ted scene thing was initially a very gradual process. However, since 2005 I have become very much part of the scene and have even got my wife involved. She often goes with me to rock and roll and Teddy Boy events. I have to say that the scene is now much smaller than it was in the seventies and eighties. This is largely because people got married and had kids and then found that they couldn't afford to go out in the same way that they had been accustomed to. The current Ted scene tends to be a lot more of a national scene although there are quite a number of rock and roll clubs to be found throughout the country. The issue as far as the Teds are concerned is that these clubs tend to be frequented and dominated by the jive bunnies or rockabillies, with only a sprinkling of local Teds. In the seventies however these clubs would have been dominated by Teds. As the eighties came in, the hepcats started to frequent these same clubs and a considerable number of people who had started out being Teds became hepcats or rockabillies. The sadness here is that these selfsame people come out with condescending comments like, 'Oh I used to be a Ted!' The irony here is that these self-same people actually believe that in being hepcat or rockabilly they have somehow grown out of being a Ted. Why?

Teddy Boys

Since becoming a Ted, I have always prided myself on being a bit of a snazzy dresser or, as some would say, 'a bit flash'. My old mother always used to say of me when I was a young boy, 'Our Nigel always looks smart, even when he goes out playing or digging the garden.' Due to the fact that I had missed out on the formation of The Edwardian Drape Society and the changes in Teddy Boy attire, I initially missed the plot dress-wise. Once I had re-established contact with my old friends in Leeds, the first thing that I realised was that I needed to get a new drape made up, albeit in a more conservative style. Since that point, I have had a considerable number of jackets and suits made up by a number of tailors which have included the late Peter Smithard in Leeds, my old tailor Keith Wilson in Leeds, Vernons (Gaelic Tailoring) in Leeds, Oakwood Tailors in Leeds, my friend Colin Taub in Hackney, East London, and I intend to go to John Anthony's in Oldham Street, Manchester who have produced some excellent suits for the Manchester Peacocks. As I am now committed to re-creating the original style, I am working towards all of my suits and jackets being of that style.

I have now become a committed Teddy Boy historian and fan of British rock and roll and since 2010 have run and produced a website called The Edwardian Teddy Boy. It is run for the benefit of all Teddy Boys and Teddy Girls who have continued to maintain this great British distinctive style and tradition. The principal aim is to promulgate the original styles of the pre-1955 Teddy Boy and actively promote the ethos and style of the original and authentic movement. Finally, in 2011, I took part in a TV Documentary called *Here Come The Teds* which came in for considerable criticism amongst the Teddy Boy movement. The saving grace for me was that a significant number of Teds told me after the documentary was televised, 'Nidge, you were one of the few people on that show who actually talked any sense!'

Interviews with Teddy Boys (2)

Where do I go from here? Well, I continue to research the history of the Teddy Boy movement, publicise the movement, drink copious quantities of Tetley Bitter and Newcastle Brown Ale, go to Ted events and just be a Ted. It is great, just great.

Appendix 1
Teddy Boys Worldwide

In the fifties and sixties, the Neo-Edwardian Teddy Boy was a uniquely British phenomenon. The youth of Continental Europe tended to follow the fashions of the US. The dominant Euro fashion of the equivalent of the Teddy Boy was quiffed hair, white T-shirt, black leather jacket, jeans and baseball boots, a style copied directly from fifties America.

However, there was a massive rock and roll revival in Europe, and especially France, in the late seventies and early eighties, parallel to the British revival of a few years earlier. Abandoning most of the Americanised style from the fifties, young French lads looked not across the Atlantic for inspiration, because there was no real fifties youth revival there, but across the English Channel, wholeheartedly embracing the style and attitude of the British seventies Ted. The French Teddy Boys had arrived, in force. Like their UK counterparts they had a reputation for violence and fought an ongoing war with black youth gangs in Paris, most notoriously the Black Panther gang. This resulted in the deaths of two French Teds in the late seventies. The 'war' only ended when the Teds and Hells Angels teamed up to take on the Black Panthers.

There is a very big Ted scene in France today. Some French Teds are very flamboyant, favouring the look and exaggerated style of the British seventies Ted. In general the French Teds are great supporters of the British movement and the British rock and roll scene, and have been since the seventies.

There is also a large and growing Teddy Boy scene in Spain, Germany, Scandinavia and in fact right across Europe and

Teddy Boys

into Russia. Adherents are commonly known as 'Euro Teds'. In Germany there is a very healthy and growing movement and they have their own bands such as the highly successful Lucifer and the Hellions. In the Republic of Ireland, the scene is starting to revive and there are well established rock and roll clubs in Dublin. Irish Teds have formed strong links with their British counterparts over the years.

The Australian equivalents of the Teddy Boys were called Bodgies, and their females the Widgies. The earliest record of the Bodgies was in 1948, some three years before the advent of the British Teds. Here again there seems to have been a quantum leap of thought that nobody can properly understand. There can be no doubt that based upon all the evidence, the entire phenomenon was a spontaneous worldwide occurrence, or what is also known as the 'hundred monkey' syndrome. This is something that the human mind cannot understand, a type of telepathy that has been around long before the invention of the internet.

The home of rock and roll music, the United States, had its equivalent of the Teddy Boy, and its own juvenile rebels are depicted in countless movies set in the fifties. A typical youth style of the time for males was a white T-shirt, black leather jacket, straight-legged jeans with turn-ups, baseball boots and a Tony Curtis haircut, and this style was copied by others around the world. Whatever the media would have us believe about the association of teenage rebellion with rock and roll music, however, the fact is that it predates rock and roll by some ten years. Some of the seminal photographs in the history of modern Western subculture were taken in the late forties, depicting hard-drinking and hard-fighting motorcycle gangs, many made up of ex-GIs who could not adjust to peacetime civilian life in California. These gangs appeared spontaneously and simultaneously, yet according to many were

Appendix 1 Teddy Boys Worldwide

unaware of each other's existence to begin with. Some of these gangs went on to morph into the Hells Angels, Pagans, Bandidos and the Outlaws motorcycle clubs in the fifties.

Sad to say, the inspirational figure of the fifties American teenage rebel, unlike the British Teddy Boy, did not prove anything like as durable in his homeland, and had completely died out in America by the mid-sixties. On an optimistic note however, when the British Teddy Boy band Furious played New York in 2011, some young American fans in the audience were seen to be wearing Teddy Boy clothing.

In Japan, rock and roll really took off in 1956. The Japanese had their Teddy Boy equivalents, known as *Tayozuku* or Sun Cult, who originally wore Hawaiian shirts and sunglasses and greased their hair back in a style known as the Shintaro after the lead character in a popular Japanese TV series of the same name. The *Tayozuku* demonstrate their love of the music and style in all the major cities every weekend, with demonstrations of their dancing in open-air public places. Today their style has evolved, and most ride motorbikes and wear all-black-leather biker suits, winkle-pickers, and have long hair combed into a large pompadour style and held in place with hair lacquer. Although to Western eyes the Japanese *Tayozuku* may appear as mad as cheese, it should be remembered that Japan is one of the most traditionally conservative cultures the modern world has ever seen, and the *Tayozuku* must be viewed in this light, and given all due credit for almost sixty years of defiance in the face of what to Western minds must be an unimaginably overwhelming cultural pressure to conform to the norms of Japanese society.

Appendix 2
A Note on the Scuttlers

The Scuttlers were gangs of vicious youths, usually between the ages of 14 and 18, who terrorised large working-class areas of Manchester between the 1860s and the 1890s. They emerged from the appalling slum dwellings of the heavily industrialised and polluted districts that encircled Manchester city centre. Each district had its own highly territorial areas that were guarded from raids by other gangs of Scuttlers. Their attire became highly distinctive. A Scuttler wore a cap worn angled towards the back of the head to display his oiled-down donkey-fringe haircut, a white muffler, a belt, bell-bottom trousers and clogs.

Fighting, or 'scuttling' as it was called, took place on a regular and often pre-arranged basis, and could involve several hundred Scuttlers. Weapons included stones and bricks, often hurled in a preliminary bombardment before the inevitable charge. Once contact with the enemy was made, a melee commenced that often lasted for hours. At close quarters the favoured weapon was the Scuttler's belt, wrapped about the wrist, with the heavy brass buckle then used to beat the opponents about the head and body. Such a belt was the Scuttler's prized possession and would often be highly personalised and decorated, perhaps with names of the Scuttler's (many) girlfriends carved on it. Knives and pokers were also ubiquitous, as was the footwear, which was always a heavy pair of pointed wooden clogs, often with small bells attached. The latter were worn so as to make as much noise as possible and added to the Scuttler's sense of bravado by announcing his arrival everywhere and to everyone. The injury rates amongst the Scuttlers were horrific, yet the police, the courts and prison appear to have had little or no deterrent effect on them or the practice of scuttling. Ex-Scuttlers often went on to become the finest rank-and-file soldiers Britain could produce.

The Scuttlers were entirely tribal in nature, fighting for the areas they lived in even though their prized territory often amounted to little more than several acres of inner-city slum. Going out and scuttling was often regarded as a far better alternative to staying at home, where several families often occupied a single, unventilated cellar or basement. Some of the most notorious gangs were the Bengal Tigers (Ancoats), the Prussia Street gang (Ancoats), the Meadow Lads (Angel Meadow), the Bradford Street gang (Ancoats), the Ordsall Lane mob (Salford), the Brown Street Lads (Salford), the Adelphi Gang (Salford), the Deansgate mob (Deansgate), the Bungall Boys (Ardwick), the Gaythorn Lads (Hulme), the Clopton Street gang (Hulme) and the Silver Street gang (Hulme). A Scuttler wandering alone into enemy territory could lose his life. They were dangerous times.

By the mid-1890s the scuttling gangs rapidly died out due to the introduction of lads' clubs, organised football, and slowly improving social and living conditions, but they remained a terrifying legend in Manchester that lasted well into the 1950s and the dawn of the Teddy Boy era. The Scuttler cult and their dress was of its time however, and like the Scuttlers themselves, will never return; unlike the cult of the Teddy Boy.

Appendix 3
Facts and Fiction

New Edwardian Teddy Boys predated rock and roll by about four years. Apart from the flat-top haircut, fifties Teds had long hair for the period, but this would be considered short by today's standards. Brylcreem was the product of choice for Ted hairstyling.

Fifties Teds did not have sideburns longer than ear-lobe length. Most were too young to grow them anyway, but for those that could, ear-lobe length was considered long, apart from the odd exception in the very late fifties. These were never of the 'lamb chop' variety, and these only came in during the late sixties and seventies. All fifties photos and text verify this fact.

Fifties Teds did not wear bright, primary-coloured drape suits. Powder blue, light grey and maroon were considered loud. There was the odd pillar-box red at the end of the fifties. This is verified by interviews with original fifties Teds.

Original Teddy Boys did not wear lots of velvet on their jackets. This was a late sixties/seventies addition and verified on all fifties photos of Teds.

Original Teddy Boys did not wear skin-tight or drainpipe trousers. Photos support the fact that high-waist, sixteen-inch trousers became tighter in the late fifties due to influence of the Italian style and in-vogue denims. This is supported by interviews and photographs.

Fifties Teddy Boys did not wear huge, two-and-a-half-inch crêpe-soled shoes. These were a later seventies addition. This is verified by interviews and photos.

Teddy Boys

Fifties Teds did not sport massive, elephant-trunk, lacquered quiffs. This is verified on all fifties photos of Teds. Huge lacquered quiffs were a seventies addition.

Teds did not wear fluorescent socks in the fifties. White, light blue, some darker colours, striped, hooped and diamond-patterned were the order of the day. This evidence is supported by interview but difficult to verify due to most fifties photographs being black and white only.

Fifties Teds did not wear winkle-picker shoes. These were a sixties and seventies phenomenon.

Fifties Teds did not wear the US-style bootlace tie with adjustable slide until the late fifties. The original bootlace tie was in fact just that; a bootlace worn under and around the shirt collar then tied under the neck in a bow.

Original early-fifties Teds did not wear the half-moon pocket style on their drapes. These, along with Bret Maverick ties, were not a British thing, they were an American style worn in the mid to late fifties (although this is possibly questionable, and photographic evidence is needed).

The overall look of the early to mid-fifties Edwardian was a classy, cultured look that can only be described as the first working-class aristocratic look. It became bastardised and ruined by the media, and by later fashions fusing with the original style, making it somewhat of a laughable parody of what it once had been. In its extreme it became virtually a cartoon rendering.

References

Books consulted include: *The Gangs of Manchester* by Andrew Davies, *The Teddy Boy as Scapegoat* by Robert J. Cross, *The Plough Boy* by Tony Parker, *The Teds* by Chris Steele-Perkins, *The Insecure Offenders* by T. R. Fyvel and *Warrior Kings* by Noel 'Razor' Smith. Other publications include *A Century Of Change: Trends in UK Statistics Since 1900* (House of Commons Research Paper: 99/111, 21 December 1999), *The Face* magazine, issue 26, June 1982, and the archives of the *Daily Mirror*.

Websites consulted include:

www.woodlands-junior.kent.sch.uk/Homework/war/rationing4.html
www.sheffieldforum.co.uk
www.everyHit.com
www.fashion-era.com
Wikipedia.org/wiki/Teddy_Boy
www.edwardianteddyboy.com
www.crazycavan.com
www.punk77.co.uk
www.historytalk.org
http://Theteddyboys.co.uk/newspaper-cuttings
www.capitalpunishmentuk.org
www.theweejun.com
http://en.wikipedia.org/wki/bodgies_and_widgies
http://en.wikipedia.org/wiki/Hells_Angels